PRINCIPLES OF TEACHING

AF670777

First published 1921
This edition published by Lector House in 2025

ISBN: 978-93-6138-545-2
Edition copyright © 2025 by Lector House LLP
All rights reserved under the International Copyright Conventions.

Every possible effort has been made to ensure that the information contained in this book is accurate at the time of going to press and the publisher cannot accept responsibility for any errors or omissions, however caused, in this unabridged, slightly corrected republication of the text of the first edition. No responsibility for loss or damage occasioned to any person, acting or refraining from action, as a result of the material in this publication can be accepted by the publisher. The publisher is not associated with any product or vendor mentioned in the book. The contents of this work are intended to further general scientific research, understanding and discussion, only. Readers should consult with a specialist, where appropriate.

No part of this publication may be reproduced, stored in a retrieval system, or transmitted, in any form, or by any means, electronic, mechanical, photocopying or otherwise, without the prior permission of the publisher.

Lector House LLP
Registered Office: H. No. 96, Block C, Tomar Colony,
Burari, Delhi – 110084, India
info@lectorhouse.com
www.lectorhouse.com

PRINCIPLES OF TEACHING

ADAM SAMUEL BENNION

2025

LECTOR HOUSE

LECTOR HOUSE LLP

PRINCIPLES OF TEACHING

BY

ADAM S. BENNION

Superintendent of Church Schools

Designed for Quorum Instructors and Auxiliary Class Teachers of the Church of Jesus Christ of Latter-day Saints.

PREFACE TO THE 1952 EDITION

Two texts have been written for the teacher training program of the Church of Jesus Christ of Latter-day Saints since Dr. Adam S. Bennion's Book *Principles of Teaching* was published, yet in spite of the fact that this book has been out of print several years so many requests for it have poured in that the General Superintendency has decided to satisfy the demand with this new edition.

This book with its classic qualities in many ways fits Shakespeare's description of a beautiful woman when he said, "Age cannot wither her nor custom dim her infinite variety." Anyone who knows Dr. Bennion or has read his writings knows that neither custom nor age has dimmed his infinite variety. Furthermore, a glance at the table of contents of this book will reveal the fact that the problems and principles treated herein are just as real today as they were when the text was written.

This little volume is republished in the hope that it again will become one of the basic texts in the teacher training program and fulfill its mission as an instrument in the hands of sincere people who have the devout wish of learning how to teach the principles of the gospel by the power of the Holy Spirit.

H.A. Dixon, Chairman
Teacher Training Committee

PREFACE

That ever-old question, "How to Teach," becomes ever new when made to read, "How to Teach Better." This volume aims to raise those problems which every teacher sooner or later faces, and it attempts to suggest an approach by way of solution which will insure at least some degree of growth towards efficiency. These chapters originally were prepared for the course offered to teacher-trainers in the Summer School of the Brigham Young University, in 1920. The teachers in that course were an inspiration to the author and are responsible for many of the thoughts expressed in the pages of this book.

The successful teacher ever views his calling as an opportunity—not as an obligation. To associate with young people is a rare privilege; to teach them is an inspiration; to lead them into the glorious truths of the Gospel of Jesus Christ is heavenly joy itself. This little volume hopes to push open the door of opportunity a little wider, that more of that joy may be realized.

"Perchance, in heaven, one day to me
Some blessed Saint will come and say,
'All hail, beloved; but for thee
My soul to death had fallen a prey';
And oh! what rapture in the thought,
One soul to glory to have brought."

ADAM S. BENNION.

CONTENTS

CHAPTER I

PURPOSES BEHIND TEACHING

OUTLINE—CHAPTER I

The worth of souls.—The Father's joy in the soul that is saved.—The teacher's responsibility.—Teaching, a sacred calling.—Our Church a teaching Church.

Our three-fold purpose in Teaching:

a—To guarantee salvation of the individual members of the Church.

b—To pass on the wonderful heritage handed down by our pioneer forefathers.

c—To make more easily possible the conversion of the world.

"Remember the worth of souls is great in the sight of God;

"For, behold, the Lord your Redeemer suffered death in the flesh; wherefore he suffered the pain of all men, that all men might repent and come unto him.

"And he hath risen again from the dead, that he might bring all men unto him, on conditions of repentance;

"And how great is his joy in the soul that repenteth.

"Wherefore, you are called to cry repentance unto this people;

"And if it so be that you should labor all your days in crying repentance unto his people, and bring, save it be one soul unto me, how great shall be your joy with him in the kingdom of my Father?

"And now, if your joy will be great with one soul that you have brought unto me into the kingdom of my Father, how great will be your joy if you should bring many souls unto me?" (Doc. & Cov., Sec. 18:10-16.)

"For behold, this is my work and my glory—to bring to pass the immortality and eternal life of man." (Moses 1:39.)

If this is the work and glory of the Lord, how great must be the responsibility of the teachers of Zion, His copartners in the business of saving humankind! Next to parenthood, teaching involves us in the most sacred relationship known to man. The teacher akin to the parent is the steward of human souls—his purpose to bless and to elevate.

The first great question that should concern the Latter-day Saint teacher is, "Why do I teach?" To appreciate fully the real purposes behind teaching is the first great guarantee of success. For teaching is "no mere job"—it is a sacred calling—a trust of the Lord Himself under the divine injunction, "Feed my sheep" (John 21:15). For the teacher who has caught a glimpse of his real responsibility there is no indifference, no eleventh-hour preparation, no feeling of unconcern about the welfare of his pupils between lessons—for him there is constant inspiration in the thought, "To me is given the privilege of being the cupbearer between the Master and His children who would drink at His fountain of truth."

The Church of Jesus Christ of Latter-day Saints has been variously designated by those not of us: "The Great Industrial Church," "The Church of Pioneers," "The Church of Wonderful Organization." It might well be called "The Teaching Church." There is scarcely a man or woman in it that has not at some time been asked to respond to the call of teacher. Our people have been a remarkable people because they have been remarkably taught—taught of the Lord and His prophets. Our future can be secure only as it is guaranteed this same good teaching. Every teacher must come to realize that "Mormonism" is at stake when he teaches. "Why do I teach?" goes to the very heart of teaching.

The answer to this question is to be found, in part at least, in the three-fold objectives of our Church. First, the salvation and exaltation of the individual soul. As already pointed out, this is the very "work and glory" of the Father. Man is born into the world a child of divinity—born for the purpose of development and perfection. Life is the great laboratory in which he works out his experiment of eternity. In potentiality, a God—in actuality, a creature of heredity, environment, and teaching. "Why do I teach?" To help someone else realize his divinity—to assist him to become all that he might become—to make of him what he might not be but for my teaching.

Someone has jocularly said: "The child is born into the world half angel, half imp. The imp develops naturally, the angel has to be cultivated." The teacher is the great cultivator of souls. Whether we say the child is half angel and half imp, we know that he is capable of doing both good and evil and that he develops character as he practices virtue and avoids vice. We know, too, that he mentally develops. Born with the capacity to do, he behaves to his own blessing or condemnation. There is no such thing as static life. To the teacher is given the privilege of pointing to the higher life. He is the gardener in the garden of life. His task is to plant and to cultivate the flowers of noble thoughts and deeds rather than to let the human soul grow up to weeds. This purpose becomes all the more significant when we realize that the effects of our teaching are not only to modify a life here of three-score and ten—they are impressions attendant throughout eternity. As the poet Goethe has said, "Life is the childhood of our immortality," and the teachings of childhood are what determine the character of maturity. The thought is given additional emphasis in the beautiful little poem, "Planting," by W. Lomax Childress:

Who plants a tree may live
To see its leaves unfold,
The greenness of its summer garb,
Its autumn tinge of gold.

Who plants a flower may live
To see its beauty grow,
The lily whiten on its stalk,
The rambler rose to blow.

Who sows the seed may find
The field of harvest fair,
The song of reapers ringing clear,
When all the sheaves are there.

But time will fell the tree,
The rose will fade and die,
The harvest time will pass away,
As does the song and sigh.

But whoso plants in love,
The word of hope and trust,
Shall find it still alive with God—
It is not made of dust.

It cannot fade nor change,
Though worlds may scattered be,
For love alone has high repose
In immortality.

If the teacher, as he stands before his class, could project his vision into the future—could see his pupils developed into manhood and womanhood, and could see all that he might do or fail to do, he would read a meaning well-nigh beyond comprehension into the question, "Why do I teach?"

A second answer to this query lies in our obligation to pass on the wonderful heritage which we here received from our pioneer forefathers. The story of their sacrifice, devotion, and achievement is unique in the history of the world. Only recently a pioneer of 1852 thrilled a parents' class in one of our wards with the simple narrative of his early experiences. His account of Indian raids, of the experience with Johnston's army, of privations and suffering, of social pastimes—all of these things rang with a spirit of romance. None of his auditors will ever forget the story of his aunt who gave up her seat in her wagon to a sick friend for whom no provision had been made, and trudged across the plains afoot that one more soul might rejoice in Zion. Every pioneer can tell this sort of thrilling story. Could our young people enjoy the companionship of these pioneers there would be little need of alarm concerning their faith. Unfortunately, each year sees fewer of these pioneers left to tell their story. It is to the teacher, both of the fireside and the classroom, that we must look for the perpetuation of the spirit of '47. The ideals and achievements of the pioneers are such an inspiration, such a challenge to the youth of the Church today—that teachers ought to glory in the opportunity to keep alive the memories of the past. Our pioneer heritage ought never to be forfeited to indifference. It is a heritage that could come only out of pioneer life. Such courage to face sacrifice, such devotion to God, such loyalty to government, such consecration to the task of conquering an unpromising and forbidding desert, such determination to secure the advantages of education, such unselfish devotion to the welfare of their fellows—where could we turn for such inspiration to one who would teach?

Nor is it enough that we strive to perfect the individual membership of the Church and preserve the social heritage out of the past—we assume to become the teachers of the world. It is our blessing to belong to a Church built upon revelation—a Church established and taught of the Lord. But with that blessing comes the injunction to carry this gospel of the kingdom to every nation and clime. "Mormonism" was not revealed for a few Saints alone who were to establish Zion—it was to be proclaimed to all the world. Every Latter-day Saint is enjoined to teach the truth. Whether called as a missionary, or pursuing his regular calling at home, his privilege and his obligation is to cry repentance and preach the plan of salvation. The better we teach, the sooner we shall make possible the realization of God's purposes in the world. The two thousand young men and women who go out each year to represent us in the ministry should go out well trained, not only that they may represent our Church as an institution which believes that "the glory of God is intelligence," but also that they may win intelligent men and women to the truth. Only he who is well taught may become a good teacher—hence the need of intelligent, devoted service. "Why do I teach?" far from being an idle question, goes to the very heart of the future of the Church.

Questions and Suggestions—Chapter I

1. How many of the members of your ward are actively engaged in other than parental teaching?
2. What significance is attached to calling our Church a teaching Church?
3. Discuss the significance of Jesus' being a teacher.
4. Compare the responsibility of teaching with that of parenthood.
5. Enumerate the chief purposes behind teaching.
6. In your opinion, which is the greatest purpose? Why?
7. To what extent does the following statement apply to the welfare of our Church:

   "That nation that does not revere its past, plays little part in the present, and soon finds that it has no future."

8. Discuss our obligation under the injunction to teach the gospel to the world.
9. Discuss the need here at home of better teaching.

10. In what sense are we trustees of the heritage left by the pioneers?

Helpful References

Doctrine & Covenants: James, *Talks on Psychology and Life's Ideals*; Brumbaugh, *The Making of a Teacher*; Weigle, *Talks to Sunday School Teachers*; Strayer, *A Brief Course in the Teaching Process*; Betts, *How to Teach Religion*; Strayer and Norsworthy, *How to Teach*; Sharp, *Education for Character*.

CHAPTER II

WHAT IS TEACHING?

OUTLINE—CHAPTER II

Teaching a complex art.—What teaching is not.—What teaching is.—What it involves.—Presentation of facts.—Organization and evaluation of knowledge.—Interpretation and elaboration of truth.—Inspiration to high ideals.—Encouragement and direction given to expression.—Discovery of pupils' better selves.—Inspiration of example as well as precept.—Application of truths taught in lives of pupils.

The query, "What constitutes teaching?" cannot be answered off-hand. It is so complex an art, so fine an art, as Professor Driggs points out, that it has to be pondered to be understood and appreciated. It is often considered to be mere lesson-hearing and lesson-giving. The difference between mere instructions and teaching is as great as the distinction between eating and digestion.

The following definition of *teaching*, contributed by a former state superintendent of schools, is rich in suggestion:

> "Teaching is the process of training an individual through the formation of habits, the acquisition of knowledge, the inculcation of ideals, and the fixing of permanent interests so that he shall become a clean, intelligent, self-supporting member of society, who has the power to govern himself, can participate in noble enjoyments, and has the desire and the courage to revere God and serve his fellows."

Teaching does not merely consist of an inquisition of questions with appropriate answers thrown in; it surely is not mere reading; nor can it be mistaken for preaching or lecturing. These are all means that may be employed in the process of teaching. And they are important, too. We have been cautioned much, of late years, not to lose ourselves in the process of doling out facts—but that rather we should occupy ourselves teaching boys and girls. That all sounds well—the writer of these lessons has himself proclaimed this doctrine—but we have discovered that you cannot teach boys and girls *nothing*. They no more can be happy *listening* to *nothing* than they can be content *doing nothing*.

And so we now urge the significance of having a rich supply of subject matter—a substantial content of lesson material. But the doctrine holds that the teacher ought not to lose himself in mere facts—they are merely the medium through which he arrives at, and drives home the truth.

> "It is the teacher's task to make changes for the better in the abilities, habits and attitudes of boys and girls. Her efficiency can be evaluated fairly only in terms of her success at this task. In other words, if a teacher is rated at all, she should be rated not only by the clothes she wears, or the method she chooses, but by the results she secures."—*Journal of Educational Research*, May, 1920.

We have said that teaching is a complex art. It consists of at least these eight fundamentals, each one of which, or any combination of which, may be featured in any one particular lesson:

1. Presentation of facts.
2. Organization and evaluation of knowledge.
3. Interpretation and elaboration of truth.
4. Inspiration to high ideals.
5. Encouragement and direction given to expression.
6. Discovery of pupils' better selves.
7. Inspiration of example as well as precept.
8. Application of truths taught in lives of the pupils.

I. Presentation of Facts

Facts constitute the background upon which the mind operates. There may be many or few—they may be presented in a lecture of thirty minutes, in the reading of a dozen pages, or they may be called forth out of the mind by a single stimulating question. But we ought not to confuse the issue. If we are to discuss any matter in the hope of reaching a conclusion in truth, we must have material upon which the mind can build that conclusion. We are not concerned in this chapter with method of procedure in getting the facts before a class—the important thought here is that the facts in rich abundance should be supplied. A certain young lady protested recently against going to Sunday School. Her explanation of her attitude is best expressed in her own words: "I get sick and tired of going to a class where I never hear anything new or worth while." Exaggerated, of course, but students are crying for bread, and ought not to be turned away with a stone.

II. Organization and Evaluation of Knowledge

We have hinted that a lesson may not have facts enough to justify the time it takes—there is, on the other hand, danger that the whole time of the class may be consumed in a mere rehearsal of facts as facts. Only recently a significant complaint was voiced by a young man who has gone through training in practically all of our organizations. "I don't seem to know anything at all," he said, "about the history of Israel, as a whole. I can recall certain isolated facts about particular persons or places, but I can't give any intelligent answer at all to such questions as these:

"Who were the Israelites? What were their big movements relative to the Promised Land? What is the history of Israel up to the time of the Savior? What is their history subsequently? Are we of Israel and how?"

The young man was not complaining—he merely regretted his ignorance on points of vital interest. He was in need of further organization of the knowledge he had. He had not been given the big central ideas about which to build the minor ones. Relative importance had not been taught him through that organized review that is so valuable in review. The teacher ought to come back time and again to pause on the big essentials—the peaks of gospel teaching.

III. Interpretation and Elaboration of Truth

It is really surprising how many various notions of an idea will be carried away by the members of a class from a single declaration on the part of a teacher. A phase of a subject may be presented which links up with a particular experience of one of the pupils. To him there is only one interpretation. To another pupil the phase of the subject presented might make no appeal at all, or linked up with a different experience might lead to an entirely different conclusion. Truths need to be elaborated and interpreted from all possible angles—all possible phases should be developed. An interesting discussion recently took place with a young man who had "gone off" on a pet doctrinal theory. His whole conception built itself up about a single passage of scripture. Satisfied with a single notion, he had shut his eyes to all else and "knew that he was right." Properly to be taught, he needed to be trained to suspend his judgment until *all the evidence* was in.

IV. Inspiration to High Ideals

Men and women like to be carried to the heights. They like to be lifted out of their lower selves into what they may become. It is the teacher's delight to let his class stand tip-toe on the facts of subject matter to peep into the glories of the gospel plan of life and salvation. In 1903 Sanford Bell, of the University of Colorado, reported the results of a survey conducted with 543 men and 488 women to ascertain whether they liked male or female teachers better and just what it was that made them like those teachers who had meant most in their lives. The survey showed that the following influences stood out in the order named:

Moral uplift.
Inspiration.
Stimulus to intellectual awakening.
Spur to scholarship.
Help in getting a firm grip on the vital issues of life.
Personal kindness.
Encouragement in crises.

What a testimonial to the force of inspiration to higher ideals!

V. Encouragement and Direction Given to Pupils' Expression

Most pupils in class are ordinarily inclined to sit silently by and let someone else do the talking. And yet, everyone enjoys participating in a lesson when once "the ice is broken." It is the teacher's task first of all to create an atmosphere of easy expression and then later to help make that expression adequate and effective. The bishop of one of our wards in southern Utah declared, not long ago, that he traced the beginning of his testimony back to a Primary lesson in which a skillful teacher led him to commit himself very enthusiastically to the notion that the Lord does answer prayers. He said he defended the proposition so vigorously that he set about to make sure from experience that he was right. The details of securing this expression will be more fully worked out in the chapter on Methods of the Recitation.

VI. Discovery of Pupils' Better Selves

One of the most fascinating problems in teaching is to come to know the real nature of our pupils—to get below surface appearances to the very boy himself. Most of the work of solving this problem necessarily must be done out of class. Such intimate knowledge is the result of personal contact when no barriers of class recitation interfere. It involves time and effort, of course, but it is really the key to genuine teaching. It makes possible what we have named as factor number eight, which may be disposed of here for present purposes. We read of bygone days largely because in them we hope to find a solution to the problems of Jimmie Livingston today. How can we effect the solution if all that we know of Jimmie is that he is one of our fifteen scouts? We must see him in action, must associate with him as he encounters his problems, if we would help him solve them. Our discovery of our pupils' better selves, and intelligent application, go together hand in hand.

VII. Inspiration of Example as Well as Precept

When Emerson declared, "What you are thunders so loudly in my ears that I can't hear what you say," he sounded a mighty note to teachers. Hundreds of boys and girls have been stimulated to better lives by the desire "to be like teacher." "Come, follow me," is the great password to the calling of teacher. The teacher conducts a class on Sunday morning—he really teaches all during the week. When Elbert Hubbard added his new commandment, "Remember the week-days, to keep them holy," he must have had teachers in mind. A student in one of our Church schools was once heard to say, "My teacher teaches me more religion by the way he plays basketball than by the way he teaches theology." It was what Jesus did that made him Savior of the world. He was the greatest *teacher* because he was the greatest man.

Surely teaching is a complex art!

Questions and Suggestions—Chapter II

1. What is teaching?
2. Why is it essential that we get a clear conception of just what teaching is?
3. Discuss the importance of building the recitation upon a good foundation of facts.
4. Why are facts alone not a guarantee of a successful recitation?
5. What is the teacher's obligation in the matter of organizing knowledge?
6. Discuss the significance of teaching as an interpretation of truth.
7. Discuss the teacher's obligation to discover pupils' better selves.
8. What is the relative importance of expression and impression in teaching?

Helpful References

Betts, *How to Teach Religion*; Gregory, *The Seven Laws of Teaching*; Thorndike, *Principles of Teaching*; Brumbaugh, *The Making of a Teacher*; Strayer and Norsworthy, *How to Teach*.

CHAPTER III

THE JOYS OF TEACHING

Outline—Chapter III

The Joys that attend Teaching: Enrichment of the spirit.—Guarantee of the teacher's own growth and development.—Restraining and uplifting influence on the moral character of the teacher.—Satisfaction that attends seeing pupils develop.—Inspirational companionship.—Contentment that attaches to duty done.—Outpouring of the blessings of the Lord.

Chapters one and two emphasized the thought that the purposes behind teaching impose a sacred obligation on the part of those who aspire to teach. But lest the obligation appear burdensome, let us remind ourselves that compensation is one of the great laws of life. "To him who gives shall be given" applies to teaching as to few other things. Verily he who loses his life finds it. The devotion of the real teacher, though it involves labor, anxiety and sacrifice, is repaid ten-fold. Only he who has fully given himself in service to others can appreciate the joy that attends teaching—particularly that teaching enjoined upon us by the Master and which is its own recompense.

It is difficult to enumerate all of the blessings that attend the service of the teacher, but let us consider a few that stand out pre-eminently.

If there were none other than this first one it would justify all that is done in the name of teaching; namely, "the enrichment of spirit." "There is a spirit in man: and the inspiration of the Almighty giveth them understanding." To feel the thrill of that inspiration is a compensation beyond price. The Lord, having commanded us to teach (see Sec. 88:77-81, Doc. & Cov.), has followed the command with the promise of a blessing, one of the richest in all scripture.

> "For thus saith the Lord, I, the Lord, am merciful and gracious unto those who fear me, and delight to honor those who serve me in righteousness and in truth unto the end;
>
> "Great shall be their reward and eternal shall be their glory;
>
> "And to them will I reveal all mysteries, yea, all the hidden mysteries of my kingdom from days of old, and for ages to come will I make known unto them the good pleasure of my will concerning all things pertaining to my kingdom;

> "Yea, even the wonders of eternity shall they know, and things to come will I show them, even the things of many generations;
>
> "And their wisdom shall be great, and their understanding reach to heaven: and before them the wisdom of the wise shall perish, and the understanding of the prudent shall come to naught;
>
> "For by my Spirit will I enlighten them, and by my power will I make known unto them the secrets of my will; yea, even those things which eye has not seen, nor ear heard, nor yet entered into the heart of man." (Doc. & Cov. 76:5-10.)

This constitutes a promissory note signed by our heavenly Father Himself. A blessing beyond compare—a dividend unfailing—and our only investment—devoted service! Companionship with the Spirit of the Lord! That is what it means, if we serve Him in faith and humility.

> "Be thou humble, and the Lord thy God shall lead thee by the hand, and give thee answer to thy prayers." (Doc. & Cov., Sec. 112:10.)

Like all other gifts and attainments, the Spirit of the Lord has to be cultivated. Teaching insures a cultivation as few other things in life can. An enriched spirit, then, is the first great reward of the teacher.

A second satisfaction is the guarantee of one's own growth and development. Teachers invariably declare that they have learned more, especially in the first year of teaching, than in any year at college. A consciousness of the fact that it is hard to teach that which is not well known incites that type of study which makes for growth. A good class is a great "pace-setter." Intellectually it has the pull of achievement. The real teacher always is the greatest student in the class. The "drive" of having a regular task to perform, especially when that task is checked up as it is by students, leads many a person to a development unknown to him who is free to slide. "Blessed is he who has to do things." Responsibility is the great force that builds character. Compare the relative development of the person who spends Tuesday evening at home with the evening paper, or at some other pastime, and of the person who, having accepted fully the call to teach, leads a class of truth-seekers through an hour's discussion of some vital subject. Follow the development through the Tuesday evenings of a lifetime.

How easy to understand that there are varying degrees of glory hereafter.

A third value of teaching lies in the fact that the position of teacher exercises a restraining influence for good on the moral life of the teacher. He is sustained by a consciousness that his conduct is his only evidence to his pupils that his practice is consistent with his theory. His class follows him in emulation or in criticism in all that he does. "Come, follow me," lifts the real teacher over the pitfalls of temptation. He cannot do forbidden work on the Sabbath, he cannot indulge in the use of tobacco, he cannot stoop to folly—his class stands between him and all these things. A teacher recently gave expression to the value of this restraining force when she said, "I urge my girls so vigorously not to go to the movies on Sunday that I find my conscience in rebellion if anyone asks me to go."

Many a man in attempting to convert another to the righteousness of a particular issue has found himself to be his own best convert. He comes to appreciate the fact that the trail he establishes is the path followed by those whom he influences. He hears the voice of the child as recorded in the little poem:

I STEPPED IN YOUR STEPS ALL THE WAY

"A father and his tiny son
Crossed a rough street one stormy day,
'See papa!' cried the little one,
'I stepped in your steps all the way!'

"Ah, random, childish hands, that deal
Quick thrusts no coat of proof could stay!
It touched him with the touch of steel—
'I stepped in your steps all the way!'

"If this man shirks his manhood's due
And heeds what lying voices say,
It is not one who falls, but two,
'I stepped in your steps all the way!'

"But they who thrust off greed and fear,
Who love and watch, who toil and pray,
How their hearts carol when they say,
'I stepped in your steps all the way!'"

Still another joy that attends teaching is the satisfaction of seeing pupils develop. The sculptor finds real happiness in watching his clay take on the form and expression of his model; the artist glories as his colors grow into life; the parent finds supreme joy in seeing himself "re-grow" in his child; so the teacher delights to see his pupils build their lives on the truths he has taught. The joy is doubly sweet if it is heightened by an expression of appreciation on the part of the pupils. Few experiences can bring the thrill of real happiness that comes to the teacher when a former student, once perhaps a little inclined to mischief or carelessness, takes him by the hand with a "God bless you for helping me find my better self."

An officer of the British army, in recounting those experiences which had come to him in the recent world war, and which he said he never could forget, referred to one which more than compensated him for all the effort he had ever put into his preparation for teaching. Because of his position in the army it became his duty to discipline a group of boys for what in the army is a serious offense. In that group was a boy who had formerly been a pupil under the officer in one of our ward organizations. Chagrin was stamped on the face of the boy as he came forward for reprimand. Regret and remorse were in the heart of the officer. They soon gave way to pride, however, as the boy assured him that worse than any punishment was the humiliation of being brought before his own teacher, and he further assured him that never again would he do a thing that would mar the sacred relations of pupil and teacher.

A further compensation attached to teaching is that of inspirational companionship. It is a blessed privilege to enjoy the sunshine of youth. Every pupil contributes an association with one of God's choice spirits. To live and work with children and adolescents is one of the finest of safeguards against old age. The teacher not only partakes of the joy of his group—they constitute him a link between his generation and theirs. Their newness of life, their optimism, their spontaneity, their joy, they gladly pass on to their teacher.

Moreover, the teacher enjoys the uplifting associations of his fellow teachers. Among those consecrated to a noble service, there is a spirit unknown to him who has not enjoyed such communion. Whether he is conscious of it or not, the teacher responds to the pull of such a group. Scores of teachers have testified that the associations they have enjoyed as members of a local board, stake board, or general board, are among the happiest of their lives.

And finally there is the contentment of mind that comes as a result of a duty well done. The human soul is so constituted that any task well performed brings a feeling of satisfaction, and this is doubly heightened when the duty performed is of the nature of a free will offering. Still more so when it is shared in by others to their blessing. Just as we hope for an eventual crowning under the blessing, "Well done, thou good and faithful servant," so we treasure those benedictions along the way that attend the discharge of a sacred obligation.

Questions and Suggestions—Chapter III

1. Quote some of the promises of the Lord to those who do His will.
2. How is teaching one of the surest guarantees of the blessings of eternal life?
3. What are the immediate joys attached to teaching?
4. Discuss the application to teaching of the truth—"He who loses his life shall find it."
5. What types of companionship are assured him who teaches?
6. As you now recall them, what distinct pleasures stand out in your teaching experience?
7. Discuss Section 76 of the Doctrine & Covenants as one of the most valuable promissory notes ever given to mankind.
8. Discuss the force of a duty done as a guarantee of joy.

Helpful References

Doctrine and Covenants: Slattery, *Living Teachers*; Sharp, *Education for Character*; Weigle, *Talks to Sunday School Teachers*; Betts, *How to Teach Religion*.

CHAPTER IV

PERSONALITY

OUTLINE—CHAPTER IV

The worth of a great teacher.—Good teachers not necessarily born.—Some boys' observations on teachers.—A high school survey.—Clapp's *Essential Characteristics*.—Betts' *Three Classes of Teachers*.—His list of qualities.

"A great teacher is worth more to a state, though he teach by the roadside, than a faculty of mediocrities housed in Gothic piles."—*Chicago Tribune*, September, 1919.

We may stress the sacred obligation of the teacher; we may discuss in detail mechanical processes involved in lesson preparation; we may analyze child nature in all of its complexity; but after all we come back to the *Personality of the Teacher* as the great outstanding factor in pedagogical success. *That something in the man* that grips people!

Very generally this *Personal Equation* has been looked upon as a certain indefinable possession enjoyed by the favored few. In a certain sense this is true. Personality is largely inherent in the individual and therefore differs as fully as do individuals. But of recent years educators have carried on extensive investigations in this field of personality and have succeeded in reducing to comprehensible terms those qualities which seem to be most responsible for achievements of successful teachers. Observation leads us all to similar deductions and constitutes one of the most interesting experiments open to those concerned with the teaching process.

Why, with the same amount of preparation, does one teacher succeed with a class over which another has no control at all?

Why is it that one class is crowded each week, while another adjourns for lack of membership?

The writer a short time ago, after addressing the members of a ward M.I.A., asked a group of scouts to remain after the meeting, to whom he put the question, "What is it that you like or dislike in teachers?" The group was a thoroughly typical group—real boys, full of life and equally full of frankness. They contributed the following replies:

1. We like a fellow that's full of pep.

2. We like a fellow that doesn't preach all the time.
3. We like a fellow that makes us be good.
4. We like a fellow that tells us new things.

Boylike, they were "strong" for pep—a little word with a big significance. Vigor, enthusiasm, sense of humor, attack, forcefulness—all of these qualities are summed up in these three letters.

And the interesting thing is that while the boys liked to be told new things, they didn't want to be preached at. They evidently had the boy's idea of preaching who characterized it as, "talking a lot when you haven't anything to say."

Still more interesting is the fact that boys like to be made to be good. In spite of their fun and their seeming indifference they really are serious in a desire to subscribe to the laws of order that make progress possible.

A principal of the Granite High School carried on an investigation through a period of four years to ascertain just what it is that students like in teachers. During those years students set down various attributes and qualities, which are summarized below just as they were given:

Desirable Characteristics

Congeniality.	Sympathy.
Broadmindedness.	Originality.
Wide knowledge.	Progressiveness.
Personality that makes discipline easy.	Effective expression.
Willingness to entertain questions.	Pleasing appearance—"good looking."
Realization that students need help.	Tact.
Sense of humor—ability to take a joke.	Patience.
Optimism—cheerfulness.	Sincerity.

Among the characteristics which they did not like in teachers they named the following:

Undesirable Characteristics

Grouchiness.	Hazy explanations.
Wandering in method.	Failure to cover assignments.
Indifference to need for help.	Distracting facial expressions.
Too close holding to the text.	Attitude of "lording it over."
Distant attitude—aloofness.	Sarcasm.
Partiality.	Poor taste in dress.
Excitability.	Bluffing—"the tables turned."
Irritability.	Discipline for discipline's sake.
Pessimism—"in the dumps."	"Holier than thouness."
Indifferent assignments.	

Desirable Capabilities

They also reduced to rather memorable phrases a half dozen desirable capabilities:

1. The ability to make students work and want to work.
2. The ability to make definite assignments.
3. The ability to make clear explanations.
4. The ability to be pleasant without being easy.
5. The ability to emphasize essentials.
6. The ability to capitalize on new ideas.
7. The ability to be human.

A number of years ago Clapp conducted a similar survey among one hundred leading school men of America, asking them to list the ten most essential characteristics of a good teacher. From the lists sent in Clapp compiled the ten qualities in the order named most frequently by the one hundred men:

1. Sympathy.
2. Address.
3. Enthusiasm.
4. Sincerity.
5. Personal Appearance.
6. Optimism.
7. Scholarship.
8. Vitality.
9. Fairness.
10. Reserve or dignity.

George Herbert Betts, in his stimulating book, *How to Teach Religion*, says there are three classes of teachers:

> "Two types of teachers are remembered: One to be forgiven after years have softened the antagonisms and resentments; the other to be thought of with honor and gratitude as long as memory lasts. Between these two is a third and a larger group: those who are forgotten, because they failed to stamp a lasting impression on their pupils. This group represents the mediocrity of the profession, not bad enough to be actively forgiven, not good enough to claim a place in gratitude and remembrance."

Mr. Betts then goes on with a very exhaustive list of positive and negative qualities in teachers—a list so valuable that we set it down here for reference.

Positive Qualities	*Negative Qualities*
1. Open-minded, inquiring, broad.	Narrow, dogmatic, not hungry for truth.
2. Accurate, thorough, discerning.	Indefinite, superficial, lazy.
3. Judicious, balanced, fair.	Prejudiced, led by likes and dislikes.
4. Original, independent, resourceful.	Dependent, imitative, subservient.

5. Decisive, possessing convictions.	Uncertain, wavering, undecided.
6. Cheerful, joyous, optimistic.	Gloomy, morose, pessimistic, bitter.
7. Amiable, friendly, agreeable.	Repellent, unsociable, disagreeable.
8. Democratic, broadly sympathetic.	Snobbish, self-centered, exclusive.
9. Tolerant, sense of humor, generous.	Opinionated, dogmatic, intolerant.
10. Kind, courteous, tactful.	Cruel, rude, untactful.
11. Tractable, co-operative, teachable.	Stubborn, not able to work with others.
12. Loyal, honorable, dependable.	Disloyal, uncertain dependability.
13. Executive, forceful, vigorous.	Uncertain, weak, not capable.
14. High ideals, worthy, exalted.	Low standards, base, contemptible.
15. Modest, self-effacing.	Egotistical, vain, autocratic.
16. Courageous, daring, firm.	Overcautious, weak, vacillating.
17. Honest, truthful, frank, sincere.	Low standards of honor and truth.
18. Patient, calm, equable.	Irritable, excitable, moody.
19. Generous, open-hearted, forgiving.	Stingy, selfish, resentful.
20. Responsive, congenial.	Cold, repulsive, uninviting.
21. Punctual, on schedule, capable.	Tardy, usually behindhand, incapable.
22. Methodical, consistent, logical.	Haphazard, desultory, inconsistent.
23. Altruistic, given to service.	Indifferent, not socially minded.
24. Refined, alive to beauty, artistic.	Coarse, lacking aesthetic quality.
25. Self-controlled, decision, purpose.	Suggestible, easily led, uncertain.
26. Good physical carriage, dignity.	Lack of poise, ill posture, no grace.
27. Taste in attire, cleanliness, pride.	Careless in dress, frumpy, no pride.
28. Face smiling, voice pleasant.	Somber expression, voice unpleasant.
29. Physical endurance, vigor, strength.	Quickly tired, weak, sluggish.
30. Spiritual responsiveness, strong.	Spiritually weak, inconstant, uncertain.
31. Prayer life warm, satisfying.	Prayer cold, formal, little comfort.
32. Religious certainty, peace, quiet.	Conflict, strain, uncertainty.
33. Religious experience expanding.	Spiritual life static or losing force.
34. God a near, inspiring reality.	God distant, unreal, hard of approach.
35. Power to win others to religion.	Influence little or negative.
36. Interest in Bible and religion.	Little concern for religion and Bible.

37. Religion makes life fuller and richer.	Religion felt as a limitation.
38. Deeply believe great fundamentals.	Lacking in foundations for faith.
39. Increasing triumph over sin.	Too frequent falling before temptation.
40. Religious future hopeful.	Religious growth uncertain.

Questions and Suggestions—Chapter IV

1. Think of the teachers who stand out most clearly in your memory. Why do they so stand out?
2. Name the qualities that made the Savior the *Great Teacher*.
3. If you had to choose between a fairly capable but humble teacher, and a very capable but conceited one, which one would be your choice? Why?
4. What is your argument against the idea, "Teachers are born, not made"?
5. Discuss the relative significance of the qualities quoted from Betts.

Helpful References

O'Shea, *Every-day Problems in Teaching*; Betts, *How to Teach Religion*; Brumbaugh, *The Making of a Teacher*; Palmer, *The Ideal Teacher*; Slattery, *Living Teachers*; Weigle, *Talks to Sunday School Teachers*.

CHAPTER V

PERSONALITY

Outline—Chapter V

The six major qualities:—a. Sympathy.—b. Sincerity.—c. Optimism.—d. Scholarly attitude.—e. Vitality.—f. Spirituality.

To set about to cultivate separate qualities would be rather a discouraging undertaking. As a matter of fact, many of the characteristics named really overlap, while others are secondary in importance. For practical purposes let us enlarge upon five or six qualities which everyone will agree are fundamental to teaching success.

The class in Teacher Training, at the Brigham Young University, in the summer of 1920, named these six as the most fundamental:

1. Sympathy.
2. Sincerity.
3. Optimism.
4. Scholarly attitude.
5. Vitality.
6. Spirituality.

No attempt was made to set them down in the order of relative importance.

1. Sympathy

This is a very broad and far-reaching term. It rests upon experience and imagination and involves the ability to live, at least temporarily, someone else's life. Sympathy is fundamentally vicarious. Properly to sympathize with children a man must re-live in memory his own childhood or he must have the power of imagination to see things through their eyes. Many a teacher has condemned pupils for doing what to them was perfectly normal. We too frequently persist in viewing a situation from our own point of view rather than in going around to the other side to look at it as our pupils see it. It is no easy matter thus "to get out of ourselves" and become a boy or girl again, but it is worth the effort.

Along with this ability at vicarious living, sympathy involves an interest in others. Sympathy is a matter of concern in the affairs of others. The rush and stir of modern life fairly seem to force us to focus our attention upon self, but if we would succeed as teachers, we must make ourselves enter into the lives of our pupils out of an interest to see how they conduct their lives, and the reasons for such conduct.

Coupled with this interest in others and the imagination to see through their eyes, sympathy involves a desire to help them. A man may have an interest in people born out of mere curiosity or for selfish purposes, but if he has sympathy for them, he must be moved with a desire to help and to bless them.

And, finally, sympathy involves the actual doing of something by way of service. President Grant liked to refer to a situation wherein a particular person was in distress. Friends of all sorts came along expressing regret and professing sympathy. Finally a fellow stepped forward and said, "I feel to sympathize with this person to the extent of fifty dollars." "That man," said President Grant, "has sympathy in his heart as well as in his purse."

2. Sincerity

Surely this is a foundation principle in teaching:

"Thou must to thyself be true,
If thou the truth would teach;
Thy soul must overflow,
If thou another soul would reach."

A teacher must really be converted to what he teaches or there is a hollowness to all that he utters. "Children and dogs," it is said, are the great judges of sincerity—they instinctively know a friend. No teacher can continue to stand on false ground before his pupils. The superintendent of one of our Sunday Schools, having selected one of the most talented persons in his ward to teach a Second Intermediate Class was astonished some months later to receive a request from the class for a change of teachers. The class could assign no specific reasons for their objections, except that they didn't get anything out of the class. A year later the superintendent learned that the teacher was living in violation of the regulations of the Church, on a particular principle, and it was perfectly clear why his message didn't ring home.

The sincere teacher not only believes what he teaches—he consecrates his best efforts to the task in hand. He urges no excuse for absence or lack of preparation—"he is there." He lets his class feel that for the time being it is his greatest concern. He meets with boys and girls because he loves to and reaches out to them with an enthusiasm that cannot be questioned.

3. Optimism

is the sunshine of the classroom. It is as natural to expect a plant to develop when covered with a blanket as it is to expect a class to be full of activity and responsiveness under an influence of unnatural solemnity. Lincoln is quoted as having declared, "You can catch more flies with a drop of honey than with a gallon of vinegar"—a homely expression, but full of suggestion. A grouch is no magnet.

A little girl when questioned why she liked her Sunday School teacher said, "Oh, she always smiles at me and says, hello." There is contagion in the cheeriness of a smile that cannot be resisted. Children live so naturally in an atmosphere of happiness and fun that teachers of religious instruction may well guard against making their work too formally sober. Frequently teachers feel the seriousness of their undertaking so keenly that they worry or discipline themselves into a state of pedagogical unnaturalness. There is very great force behind the comment of the student who appreciated the teacher who could be human. The experience is told of a teacher who continued to have difficulty with one of her pupils. He so persisted in violating regulations that he was kept in after school regularly, and yet after school hours he was one of the most helpful lads in the school; in fact, he and the teacher seemed almost chummy. Struck by the difference in his attitude, the teacher remarked to him one afternoon, as he went about cleaning the blackboard, "Jimmie, I have just been wondering about you. You're one of my best workers after school—I can't understand how you can be so different during school hours and after."

"Gee, that's funny," put in Jimmie, "I was just thinking the same thing about you."

To be cheerful without being easy is a real art. Liberty is so often converted into license, and a spirit of fun so easily transformed into mischief and disorder. And yet cheerfulness is the great key to the human heart.

An attitude of looking for the good in pupils will lead to a response of friendliness on their part which is the basis of all teaching.

4. Scholarly Attitude

If a teacher would cultivate an appetite for learning among his pupils he must himself hunger for knowledge. Most young people will "take intellectually if sufficiently exposed." A scholarly attitude implies first of all a growing mastery of subject matter. To quote an eminent writer on religious education, "A common bane of Sunday school teaching has been the haziness of the teacher's own ideas concerning the truths of religion."

Fancy the hostess who would invite her guests to a dinner, and upon their arrival indicate to them that she had made only vague plans to receive them. No special place for their wraps, no entertainment for their amusement, and then fancy her asking them to sit down to a warmed-up conglomeration of left-overs.

Of course, it is only in fancy that we can imagine such a service. Yet reports frequently indicate that there are class recitations, intellectual banquets, for which the preparation has been about as meagre as that indicated. Surely he who would feast others upon His word should prepare unceasingly. Let us keep in mind the comment—"We like the fellow who tells us something new."

Along with this mastery of subject matter, a scholarly attitude implies both broadmindedness and openmindedness. Seekers after truth should welcome it from all available sources, and ought not to be handicapped by bias or prejudice.

Tolerance and a willingness to entertain questions—a constant effort to view a subject from every possible angle—a poise that attends self-control even under stress of annoyance—these things are all involved in a truly scholarly attack upon any given problem.

5. Vitality

One of the qualities most favorably and frequently commented on by students is what they call "pep." A certain vigor of attack that seems to go directly to the point at stake, putting at rest all other business and making discipline unnecessary, is what twentieth century young people seem to like. The element of hero worship prompts them to demand that the leader shall "do things." They like the "push" that takes a man over the top, the drive that wins a ball game, the energy that stamps the business man with success. Vitality is an inherent factor in leadership.

6. Spirituality

The crowning glory of the successful religious teacher is that spiritual glow which links up heaven and earth.

> "And the Spirit shall be given unto you by the power of faith, and if ye receive not the Spirit, ye shall not teach." (Doc. & Cov., Sec. 42:14.)

This divine injunction is given us because we have undertaken to teach His Gospel. We would lead others to Him. And this is possible only as we lead by the light of His Holy Spirit. Above our knowledge of facts and our understanding of child nature must be placed our communion with that Spirit which touches the hearts of men.

If a teacher would prepare a young man for a place in a modern business house he must teach him the ways of business,—buying, selling, collecting, managing, etc.,—matters of fact, governed by the laws of barter and trade. If that same teacher would teach the same young man the way of eternal life, he must substitute for the laws of man the word of the Lord, and for the spirit of exchange, the Spirit of Heaven. A pupil can be prepared for the kingdom of God only as he is led to respond to and appreciate His Spirit, and to do His will. While it is true that the best way to prepare for heaven is to live the best possible life here on earth, yet we need the Spirit of the Lord to interpret what constitutes that best possible life.

There is power in the intellect of man; there is glory in that power when it is heightened by the Spirit of the Almighty.

Questions and Suggestions—Chapter V

1. What is sympathy?

2. Why is it so essential in teaching?
3. Why is sincerity a foundation principle in all teaching?
4. Discuss the obligation on the part of the teacher to leave his troubles outside the classroom.
5. Discuss the statement—"Cheerfulness is spiritual sunshine."
6. Illustrate the value of cheerfulness.
7. What is the significance of the term, scholarly attitude?
8. Just what constitutes vitality?
9. Show how it is essential to teaching.
10. Why name spirituality as the crowning characteristic of the good teacher?

Helpful References

Those listed in Chapter IV.

CHAPTER VI

ATTAINMENT

Outline—Chapter VI

The possibility of growth in teaching.—How to develop spirituality: a. By cultivating the spirit of prayer; b. By leading a clean life; c. By obeying the principles of the Gospel; d. By performing one's duty in the Church; e. By reading and pondering the word of the Lord.—How to develop other qualities: a. By taking a personal inventory; b. By coming in contact with the best in life through reading and companionship; c. By forming the habit of systematic study; d. By assuming responsibility.

While we may agree as to what constitutes the desirable characteristics in teachers it is far easier to name them than to attain them. We have already pointed out that teaching is a complex art proficiency in which is the result of a long, painstaking process. But success in teaching as in all other pursuits is possible of achievement. We have heard so frequently that teachers must be born, not made, that many prospective teachers, feeling that they have been denied this pedagogical birthright, give up in despair. Of course, it is naturally easy for some individuals to teach—they do seem born possessed of a teaching personality, but they are not given a monopoly on the profession.

The Lord has too many children to be taught to leave their instruction to a few favored ones. The qualities listed in chapter five may be developed, in varying degrees, of course, by any normal person anxious to serve his fellows. The "will to do" is the great key to success.

To him who would develop spiritually, these five suggestions may be helpful:

First, cultivate the spirit of prayer. The president of one of our stakes made the remark once that he believed only a few of the men and women of his stake really pray. "They go through the form, all right," he said; "they repeat the words—but they do not enter into the spirit of the prayer. If the Lord doesn't draw nearer to them than they do to Him I doubt that their prayers are really of very great force."

The ability to pray is the great test of a spiritual life. "The faith to pray" is a gift to be cultivated through devoted practice. The teacher who would have his pupils draw nearer to him must himself draw near to the Lord. The promise, "Ask, and ye shall receive, seek, and ye shall find," was given only to those who ask in faith.

This constant prayer of faith, then is the first great guarantee of the Spirit.

The second is a clean life. Just as it is impossible for water to make its way through a dirty, clogged pipe, so it is for the Spirit to flow through a channel of unrighteous desires. A visitor was interested a short time ago in Canada in attempting to get a drink out of a pipe that had been installed to carry water from a spring in the side of a mountain to a pool at the side of the road. Due to neglect, moss and filth had been allowed to collect about the bottom of the pipe, until it was nearly choked up. Getting a drink was out of the question. And yet there was plenty of water in the spring above—just as fine water as had ever flowed from that source. It was simply denied passage down to those who would drink. And so with the Spirit. The Lord is still able to bless—all too frequently, we so live that "the passage is clogged." The Word of Wisdom is not only a guarantee of health—it is the key to communication with the Spirit. And what is true of the body applies with even greater force to cleanliness of mind. The teacher might well adopt this prayer:

> "Create in me a clean heart, O God, and renew a right spirit within me."

The third great guarantee of the Spirit is an unswerving obedience to all principles of the Gospel. To teach belief a man must believe. Firmly grounded in all the cardinal principles the teacher may well inspire a spirit of the Gospel, but not otherwise. Doubt and uncertainty will keep the teacher from the position of counsel and leadership.

The fourth assurance in the matter of developing spirituality is the consistent performance of one's religious obligations. The complaint is often made that teachers in a particular organization will meet their classes regularly, but that done they seem to consider their religious duties discharged. Teaching does not excuse a person from attending the other services required of Latter-day Saints. He is asked to attend Sacrament meetings, Priesthood meetings, Union meetings, special preparation meetings—they are all essential to the full development of the Spirit of the Gospel, which is the spirit of teaching. The teacher may rightly expect to be sustained only as he sustains those who preside over him.

> "For with what judgment ye judge, ye shall be judged: and with what measure ye mete, it shall be measured to you again." (Matt. 7:2.)

And finally, if we would enjoy the spirit of our work we must familiarize ourselves with the Word of the Lord. To read it is to associate in thought with Him. His Spirit pervades all that He has said, whether in ancient or modern times. One of our apostles frequently remarked that if he would feel fully in touch with the spirit of his calling he must read regularly from the Doctrine & Covenants. "That book keeps me attuned as no other book can." It is not given to us to associate here with the Master, but through His recorded words we can live over all that He once lived. Thereby we not only come really to know what He would have us do, we partake of a spirit that surpasses understanding.

> "Search the scriptures, for in them ye think ye have eternal life."

As for attainment in other matters involved in the teaching process, the teachers who attended the course at the Brigham Young University were agreed that regular practice in the following processes will insure marked growth and development:

1. The taking of a personal inventory at regular intervals. "Am I the kind of teacher I should like to go to?" starts an investigation full of suggestiveness. The qualities listed in chapter four constitute a reference chart for analysis. A teacher can become his own best critic if he sets up the proper ideals by way of a standard. A teacher in one of our Church schools in Idaho carried out an interesting investigation during the year 1919-1920. Anxious that he should not monopolize the time in his recitations, he asked one of his students to tabulate the time of the class period as follows:

Number of questions asked by teacher.
Number of questions asked by pupils.
Amount of time consumed by teacher.
Amount of time consumed by pupils.

He was astonished to discover that of the forty-five minutes given to recitation he was regularly using an average of thirty-two minutes. Similar investigations can be carried on by any interested teacher.

2. Contact with the best in life. It is a fundamental law in life that life is an adaptation to environment. The writer has been interested in observing the force of this law as it affects animal life. Lizards in Emery county are slate-gray in color that they may be less conspicuous on a background of clay and gray sandstone; the same animals in St. George take on a reddish color—an adaptation to their environment of red sandstone.

Nor is the operation of this law merely a physical process. On a trip into Canada recently the writer traveled some distance with a group of bankers in attendance at a convention at Great Falls. On his way home he took a train on which there was a troupe of vaudeville players. The contrast was too marked to escape notice. One group had responded to an environment of sober business negotiations—the other to the gayety of the footlights. And so the teacher who would grow must put himself into an environment that makes the kind of growth he desires natural—inevitable. Through good books he can associate with the choice spirits of all ages. No one denies his acquaintanceship. Great men have given their best thoughts to many of the problems that confront us. We can capitalize on their wisdom by reading their books. We re enforce ourselves with their strength.

Magazines, too, are full of stimulation. They constitute a kind of intellectual clearing house for the best thought of the world today. Business houses value them so highly in promoting the advancement of their employees that they subscribe regularly. One manager remarked: "No one factor makes for greater growth among my men than reading the achievements of others—leaders in their lines—through the magazines." There is scarcely a phase of life which is not being fully written about in the current issues of the leading magazines.

Then, too, contact with men and women of achievement is a remarkable stimulus to growth.

There are leaders in every community—men and women rich in experience—who will gladly discuss the vital issues of life with those who approach them. There still remain, too, pioneers with their wonderful stories of sacrifice and devotion. To the teacher who will take the pains there is an untold wealth of material in the lives of the men and women about him.

3. Regular habits of systematic study. Thorough intensive effort finds its best reward in the intellectual growth that it insures. In these days of the hurry of business and the whirl of commercialized amusements there is little time left for study except for him who makes himself subscribe to a system of work. Thirty minutes of concentrated effort a day works wonders in the matter of growth. President Grant was a splendid evidence of the force of persistent effort in his writing, his business success, and his rise to the leadership of half a million Latter-day Saints.

4. Assuming the obligations of responsibility. In every organization there are constant calls upon teachers to perform laborious tasks. It is so natural to seek to avoid them—so easy to leave them for somebody else—that we have to cultivate vigorously a habit of accepting the obligations that present themselves. The difficulties of responsibility are often burdensome, but they are an essential guarantee of achievement. "Welcome the task that makes you go beyond your ordinary self, if you would grow!"

Questions and Suggestions—Chapter VI

1. Discuss our obligation to grow.
2. Point out the difference between praying and merely saying prayers.
3. Discuss the various means which guarantee spiritual growth.
4. Comment on the thought that a personal inventory is as essential to teaching as it is to financial success.
5. What is your daily scheme for systematic study?
6. What plan do you follow in an attempt to know the scriptures?
7. Why is it so important that we assume the responsibilities placed upon us?

Helpful References

Those listed in Chapter IV.

CHAPTER VII

NATIVE TENDENCIES

OUTLINE—CHAPTER VII

Importance of Child Study to teachers.—Teaching both a social and an individual process.—A Child's characteristics—his birthright.—What the nervous system is.—Types of original responses.—The significance of instinctive action.—Colvin's list of native tendencies.—Sisson's list.—A knowledge of native tendencies essential to proper control of human behavior.

We have now discussed the significance and meaning of teaching, together with the consideration of the characteristics that constitute the personal equation of the teacher. It is now pertinent that we give some attention to the nature of the child to be taught, that we may the more intelligently discuss methods of teaching, or how teacher and pupil get together in an exchange of knowledge.

Teaching is a unique process. It is both social and individual. The teacher meets a class—a collection of pupils in a social unit. In one way he is concerned with them generally—he directs group action. But in addition to this social aspect, the problem involves his giving attention to each individual in the group. He may put a general question, but he gets an individual reply. In short, he must be aware of the fact that his pupils, for purposes of recitation, are all alike; and at the same time he must appreciate the fact that they are peculiarly different. In a later chapter we shall consider these differences; let us here consider the points of similarity.

The fact that a boy is a boy makes him heir to all of the characteristics that man has developed. These characteristics are his birthright. He responds in a particular way to stimuli because the race before him has so responded. There is no need here of entering into a discussion as to how great a controlling factor heredity may be in a man's life, or how potent environment may be in modifying that life—we are concerned rather with the result—that man is as he is. It is essential that we know his characteristics, particularly as they manifest themselves in youth, so that we may know what to expect in his conduct and so that we may proceed to modify and control that conduct. Just as the first task of the physician is to diagnose his case—to get at the cause of the difficulty before he proceeds to suggest a remedy—so the first consideration of the teacher is a query, "Whom do I teach?"

Man may normally be expected to respond in a particular way to a particular stimulus because men throughout the history of the race have so responded. Certain connections have been established in his nervous system and he acts accordingly—he does what he does because he is *man*. We cannot here go into a detailed discussion of the physiological processes involved in thinking and other forms of behavior, but perhaps we may well set down a statement or two relative to man's tendencies to act, and their explanations:

> "The nervous system is composed of neurones of three types: Those that receive, the afferent; those that effect action, the efferent; and those that connect, the associative. The meeting places of these neurones are the synapses. All neurones have the three characteristics of sensitivity, conductivity, and modifiability. In order for conduct or feeling or intellect to be present, at least two neurones must be active, and in all but a few of the human activities many more are involved. The possibility of conduct or intelligence depends upon the connections at the synapses,—upon the possibility of the current affecting neurones in a certain definite way. The possession of an 'original nature,' then, means the possession, as a matter of inheritance, of certain connections between neurones, the possession of certain synapses which are in functional contact and across which a current may pass merely as a matter of structure. Just why certain synapses should be thus connected is the whole question of heredity. Two factors seem to affect the functional contact of a synapses,—first, proximity of the neurone ends, and second, some sort of permeability which makes a current travel on one rather than another of two neurones equally near together in space. This proximity and permeability are both provided for by the structure and constitution of the nervous system. It should be noted that the connection of neurones is not a one-to-one affair, but the multiplicity of fibrils provided by original nature makes it possible for one afferent to discharge into many neurones, and for one efferent neurone to receive the current from many neurones. Thus the individual when born is equipped with potentialities of character, intellect and conduct, because of the pre-formed connections or tendencies to connections present in his nervous system.
>
> "*Types of Original Responses.*—These unlearned tendencies which make up the original nature of the human race are usually classified into automatic or physiological actions, reflexes, instincts, and capacities. Automatic actions are such as those controlling the heart-beats, digestive and intestinal movements; the contraction of the pupil of the eye from light, sneezing, swallowing, etc., are reflexes; imitation, fighting, and fear, are instincts, which capacities refer to those more subtle traits by means of which an individual becomes a good linguist, or is tactful, or gains skill in handling tools. However, there is no sharp line of division between these various unlearned tendencies; what one

psychologist calls a reflex or a series of reflexes, another will call an instinct. It seems better to consider them as of the same general character but differing from each other in simplicity, definiteness, uniformity of response, variableness among individuals, and modifiability. They range from movements such as the action of the blood vessels to those concerned in hunting and collecting; from the simple, definite, uniform knee-jerk, which is very similar in all people and open to very little modification, to the capacity for scholarship, which is extremely complex, vague as to definition, variable both as to manifestation in one individual and amounts amongst people in general, and is open to almost endless modification. This fund of unlearned tendencies is the capital with which each child starts, the capital which makes education and progress possible, as well as the capital which limits the extent to which progress and development in any line may proceed." *The Psychology of Childhood*, pp. 21, 22, 23.

Weigle, in his *Talks to Sunday School Teachers,* begins his second chapter in a rather unique and helpful manner relative to this same question:

> "The little human animal, like every other, is born going. He is already wound up. His lungs expand and contract; his heart is pumping away; his stomach is ready to handle food. These organic, vital activities he does not initiate. They begin themselves. The organism possesses them by nature. They are the very conditions of life.
>
> "There are many other activities, not so obviously vital as these, for which nature winds him up quite as thoroughly—yes, and sets him to go off at the proper time for each. He will suck when brought to the breast as unfailingly as his lungs will begin to work upon contact with the air. He will cry from hunger or discomfort, clasp anything that touches his fingers or toes, carry to his mouth whatever he can grasp, in time smile when smiled at, later grow afraid when left alone or in the dark, manifest anger and affection, walk, run, play, question, imitate, collect things, pull things apart, put them together again, take pleasure in being with friends, act shy before strangers, find a chum, belong to a 'gang' or 'bunch,' quarrel, fight, become reconciled, and some day fall in love with one of the opposite sex. These, and many more, are just his natural human ways. He does not of purpose initiate them any more than he initiates breathing or heart-beat. He does these things because he is so born and built. They are his instincts."

As Norsworthy and Whitley point out, we are not especially concerned with the boundary lines between automatic actions, reflexes, and instincts—we are rather concerned with the fact that human beings possess native tendencies to act in particular ways. Some psychologists stress them as instincts; others as capacities, but they have all pretty generally agreed that under certain stimuli there are natural tendencies to react.

These tendencies begin to manifest themselves at birth—they are all potentialities with the birth of the child—and continue to develop in turn, certain ones being more pronounced in the various stages of the child's life. Colvin in his *The Learning Process*, runs through the complete list of possibilities. According to him man, in a lifetime, is characterized by the following tendencies: Fear, anger, sympathy, affection, play, imitation, curiosity, acquisitiveness, constructiveness, self-assertion (leadership), self-abasement, rivalry, envy, jealousy, pugnacity, clannishness, the hunting and predatory instincts, the migratory instinct, love of adventure and the unknown, superstition, the sex instincts, which express themselves in sex-love, vanity, coquetry, modesty; and, closely allied with these, the love of nature and of solitude, and the aesthetic, the religious, and the moral emotions.

Sisson, in a little book that every teacher ought to know, *The Essentials of Character*, emphasizes the importance for teaching of ten tendencies: bodily activity, sense-hunger and curiosity, suggestibility, tastes and aesthetic appreciation, self-assertion, love, joy, fear, the growing-up impulse, the love of approbation.

As already indicated, the teacher should give attention to these tendencies that he may the better know how to proceed. If he knows that the one great outstanding impulse of a boy of seven is to do something, he perhaps will be less likely to plan an hour's recitation on the theory that for that hour the boy is to do nothing. If he knows that one of the greatest tendencies of boys from ten to fourteen is to organize "gangs" for social and "political" purposes, he will very likely capitalize on this idea in building up a good strong class spirit.

Knowing that children naturally respond to certain stimuli in very definite ways, the teacher can better set about to furnish the right stimuli—he can be in a better position to *direct and control behavior*.

Questions and Suggestions—Chapter VII

1. What significance attaches to the statement, "Children are born 'going'"?
2. Why is it of vital importance that teachers give attention to the native tendencies in children?
3. What constitutes instinctive action? Illustrate.
4. Name the instincts that are essentially individualistic. Those that are essentially social.
5. What native tendencies are of most concern to teachers?
6. Discuss the relative significance of heredity, environment, and training in the development of children.
7. To what extent is a child limited in its development by its nervous system?

Helpful References

Norsworthy and Whitley, *The Psychology of Childhood*; Weigle, *Talks to Sunday School Teachers*; Colvin, *The Learning Process*; Sisson, *The Essentials of Character*; Stiles, *The Nervous System and its Conservation*; Thorndike, *Principles of Teaching*; Harrison, *A Study of Child Nature*; Kirkpatrick, *Fundamentals of Child Study*.

CHAPTER VIII

"WHAT TO DO WITH NATIVE TENDENCIES"

OUTLINE—CHAPTER VIII

Characteristic tendencies of the various stages of child life.—The teacher's attitude toward them.—Follow the grain.

Four methods of procedure: 1. The method of disuse; 2. The method of rewards and punishment; 3. The method of substitution; 4. The method of stimulation and sublimation.

Having listed the native tendencies generally, we might well now consider them as they manifest themselves at the various stages of an individual's development. As already indicated, they constitute his birthright as a human being, though most of them are present in the early years of his life only in potentiality. Psychologists of recent years have made extensive observations as to what instincts are most prominent at given periods. Teachers are referred particularly to the volumes of Kirkpatrick, Harrison, and Norsworthy and Whitley. In this latter book, pages 286, 287, and 298-302, will be found an interesting tabulation of characteristics at the age of five and at eleven. For the years of adolescence Professor Beeley, in his course at the Brigham Young Summer School, in the Psychology of Adolescence, worked out very fully the characteristics unique in this period, though many of them, of course, are present at other stages:

CHARACTERISTICS UNIQUE IN THE ADOLESCENT PERIOD

1. Maturing of the sex instincts.
2. Rapid limb growth.
3. Over-awkwardness.
4. Visceral organs develop rapidly (heart, liver, lungs, genital organs.)
5. Change in physical proportions; features take on definite characteristics.
6. Brain structure has matured.
7. Self-awareness.
8. Personal pride and desire for social approval.
9. Egotism.
10. Unstable, "hair-trigger," conflicting emotions.

11. Altruism, sincere interest in the well-being of others.
12. Religious and moral awakening.
13. New attitude.
14. Aesthetic awakening.
15. Puzzle to everybody.
16. Desire to abandon conventionalities, struggle for self-assertion.
17. Career motive.
18. Period of "palling" and mating; clique and "gang" spirit.
19. Positiveness,—affirmation, denial.
20. Inordinate desire for excessive amusement.
21. Evidence of hereditary influences.
22. "Hero worship," castle building.
23. "Wanderlust."
24. Hyper-suggestibility.
25. Ideals; ambitions.
26. Yearning for adult responsibility.

Having listed these tendencies we still face the question, "What shall we do with them? What is their significance in teaching?"

It is perfectly clear, in the first place, that we ought not to ignore them. None of them is wholly useless, and few of them can safely be developed just as they first manifest themselves. They call for training and direction.

> "Some instincts are to be cherished almost as they are; some rooted out by withholding stimuli, or by making their exercise result in pain or discomfort, or by substituting desirable habits in their place; most of the instincts should be modified and redirected."—(*Thorndike.*)

Our concern as teachers ought to be that in our work with boys and girls, men and women, we are aware of these natural tendencies that we may work with them rather than contrary to them—that we may "follow the grain" of human nature.

Since these tendencies are the result of responses to stimuli they may be modified by attention either to the stimuli or to the reaction that attends the stimulation. Four methods call for our consideration:

1. The method of disuse.
2. The method of rewards and punishments.
3. The method of substitution.
4. The method of stimulation and sublimation.

No one of these methods can be said always to be best. The nature of the person in question, his previous experience and training, together with the circumstances attending a given situation, all are factors which determine how we should proceed. The vital point is, that both as parents and teachers we should guard against falling into the rut of applying the same treatment to all cases regardless of their nature.

1. The Method of Disuse

This method is largely negative. It aims to safeguard an individual against ills by withholding stimuli. The mother aims to keep scissors out of reach and sight of the baby that it may not be lured into danger. Some parents, upon discerning that the pugnacious instinct is manifesting itself vigorously in their boy, isolate him from other boys—keep him by himself through a period of a year or more that the tendency may not be accentuated. Other parents, observing their daughter's inclination to be frivolous, or seeing the instinct of sex begin to manifest itself in her interest in young men, send her away to a girl's school—a sort of intellectual nunnery.

Frequently teachers follow this method in the conduct of their classes. The tendency to self-assertion and verbal combat, natural to youth, is smothered by an unwillingness on the part of the teacher to indulge questions and debate or by a marked inclination to do all the talking.

It is clear that this method of disuse has its place in the training of children, though grave dangers attend its too frequent indulgence. Children and others of immature judgment need the protection of withheld stimuli. But clearly this is not a method to be recommended for general application. The boy who is never allowed to quarrel or fight may very possibly grow up to be a man afraid to meet the battles of life; the girl, if her natural emotions are checked, may lose those very qualities that make for the highest type of womanhood and motherhood. Fortunately, in these days, it is pretty nearly impossible to bring boys and girls up in "glass houses." Doubly fortunate, for they are made happy in their bringing up and are fitted for a world not particularly devoted to the fondling of humankind.

2. The Method of Rewards and Punishments

This method is clearly illustrated in the training of "trick" animals. These creatures through innumerable repetitions are made to do phenomenal "stunts." In the training for every successful "try" they are rewarded with a cube of sugar, a piece of candy, or some other pleasure-producing article; for every miss they are punished—made to suffer pain or discomfort. This same sort of procedure carries over into human affairs. Witness the hickory stick and the ruler, or count the nickels and caresses. Ridicule before the class, and praise for commendable behavior or performance, are typical of this same method. If it is followed, and it clearly has a place in the training of children, care should be exercised to see that in the child's mind in any case there is clear connection between what he has done and the treatment that he receives. With some parents it fairly seems as if their one remedy for all offences is a tingling in the epidermis—it is equally clear that with some teachers their one weapon is sarcasm. All too frequently these measures grow out of unsettled nerves or stirred up passions, on the part of the parent or teacher, and have really but little connection—remote at best—with the offense in question. There may be an abuse in the matter of rewards, too, of course, but as a rule few classes suffer from too much appreciation. The real art of discipline lies in making the reward or the punishment naturally grow out of the conduct indulged in.

3. The Method of Substitution

Because of the fact that some stimuli inevitably lead to discomfort and disaster—that some conduct is bad—there is need of a method of substitution. The child's mind needs to be led from the contemplation of an undesirable course of action to something quite different. Frequently a child cannot be satisfied with a mere denial, and circumstances may not be favorable to punishment—yet the correction must be made. Substitution is the avenue of escape. A striking illustration in point occurred recently in a cafe in Montana. A trio of foreigners, father, mother, and two-year-old son, came in and sat down at one of the tables. Soon after the parents began to eat, the child caught sight of a little silver pitcher for which he began to beg. Whining and crying, mixed in with the begging, created a good bit of disturbance. The only attempted solution on the part of the parents was a series of: "Don't do that!" "No! no!" "Keep quiet, Marti!" a continued focusing of the child's attention on what he ought not to do, and an added note to the disturbance. Then an American across the aisle having surveyed the situation took out of his pocket a folder full of brightly colored views. The charm worked beautifully—the meal went on free from disturbance—and the child was happy.

This method involves a good bit of resourcefulness, calling at times for what seems an impossible amount of ingenuity. As someone has said, "It is beating the other fellow to it." It merits the consideration of those who have to handle boys and girls who are regularly up to "stunts."

4. The Method of Stimulation and Sublimation

This method is rather closely akin to that of substitution, with the exception that it capitalizes on tendencies already in operation and raises them to a higher level. Stimulation, of course, merely means the bringing of children into contact with desirable stimuli on every possible occasion; in fact, it involves the making of favorable occasions.

Sublimation involves building upon native tendencies to an elevated realization. Educationally this method is most full of promise. It is seen in kindergarten methods when a child is led from mere meaningless playing with toys to constructive manipulation of blocks, tools, etc. It is seen admirably in football where the pugnacious tendency of boys is capitalized on to build manliness in struggle and to develop a spirit of fair play. It is seen in the fostering of a girl's fondness for dolls, so that it may crystallize into the devotion of motherhood. It is seen when a boys' man leads a "gang" of boys into an association for social betterment. It is seen when a teacher works upon the instinct to collect and hoard, elevating it into a desire for the acquisition of knowledge and the finer things of life.

Whatever our method, let us give due consideration to the natural inclinations and aptitudes of boys and girls—let us help them to achieve fully their own potentialities.

Questions and Suggestions—Chapter VIII

1. Point out the essential differences between boys and girls at the age of six and seven and those of sixteen and seventeen.
2. Discuss the significance of the following phrase: "The grain in human nature."
3. How can the hunting instinct be appealed to in religious stimulation?
4. Of what significance is the "gang spirit" to teachers of adolescents?
5. How can rivalry be made an asset in teaching?
6. How can the fighting instinct in children best be directed?
7. Why is biography so valuable in material for teaching?
8. Why is it so essential that we put responsibility upon boys and girls? How should this fact affect teaching?
9. What are the dangers that attend an attempt to keep children quiet for any length of time?

Helpful References

Those listed in Chapter VII.

CHAPTER IX

INDIVIDUAL DIFFERENCES

Outline—Chapter IX

Fundamental significance of individual differences.—Typical illustration.—The truth illustrated physically; in range of voice, in speed, in mental capabilities.—The same truth applied spiritually.—Some cases in point.

Everybody is like everybody else in this—that everybody is different from everybody else. Having discussed how all men enjoy a common heritage by way of native endowments, let us now turn to a consideration of how men differ.

Two of the terms most frequently met in recent educational publications are statistical methods and individual differences. There is nothing particularly new in this latter term—it merely represents a new emphasis being given to the old idea that no two of us are alike. Every parent is aware of the very marked differences in his children. Even twins differ in disposition and mental capabilities. In fact, one of the difficulties that attaches to parenthood is just this problem of making provision in one household for such various personalities.

A member of the stake presidency in one of the stakes in southern Utah, in discussing this matter a short time ago, remarked that in his family of four boys one very definitely had decided to become a farmer and was already busy at getting acquainted with the details of the work; a second boy was devoted to music and voiced a very vigorous protest against farming; the third son was so bashful and reticent that he hadn't given expression to any notion of preference; the fourth, a happy-go-lucky sort of chap, free and noisy in his cutting up about the place, wasn't worrying about what he was to do in life—he just didn't want anything to do with strenuous effort.

"How can I drive a four-horse team such as that?" was the interesting query of this father.

Practically every family presents this variety of attitude and practically every parent is trying to work out a solution to the problem, so there is nothing startling about the term individual differences. Educators have just given the matter more careful and scholarly attention of recent years.

If the matter of differences in children constitutes a problem of concern in a family of from two to ten children, how much greater must that problem be in a class from thirty to fifty with approximately as many families represented. The problem has led to some very interesting investigations—investigations so simple that they can be carried on by anyone interested. For instance, if we could line up all the men in Salt Lake City according to size we should find at one end of the line a few exceptionally tall men, likely from six feet to six feet six inches in height. At the other end of the line would be a few exceptionally small men—undersized men from three feet eight or ten inches to four feet six inches. In between these two types would come in graduated order all sorts of men with a decidedly large number standing about five feet six or eight inches. This latter height we call the average.

Practically we see the significance of these differences. No manufacturer thinks of making one size of overall in the hope that it will fit each of these men. He adapts his garment to their size, and he knows approximately how many of each size will be called for in the course of ordinary business.

If these same men could be taken one by one into a music studio and have their voices tested for range, the same interesting variations would be found. There would be a few very high tenors, a few exceptionally low bassos, and a crowd with medium range with fillers-in all along the line.

If we were interested in carrying the experiment still further we might apply the speed test. In a 100-yard dash a few men would be found to be particularly fast, a few others would trail away behind at a snail's pace, while the big crowd of men would make the distance in "average time."

Of course, it would be foolish to attempt to make tenors of all these men—equally foolish to try to make speeders of them all. In these practical matters we appreciate the wisdom of letting each man fit into that niche for which he is qualified.

Nor are these differences confined to the field of physical characteristics and achievements. Tests by the hundred have demonstrated beyond all question that they hold equally well of mental capabilities. In the past children have gone to school at the age of six. They have remained there because they were six. At seven they were in grade two, and so on up through the grades of our public schools. Tests and measurements now, however, are showing that such a procedure works both a hardship and an injustice on the pupils. Some boys at six are found as capable of doing work in grade two as other boys at eight. Some boys and girls at six are found wholly incapable of doing what is required in grade one. One of the most promising prospects ahead educationally is that we shall be able to find out just the capacity of a child regardless of his age, and fit him into what he can do well, making provisions for his passing on as he shows capability for higher work. Not only has this matter of individual differences been found to apply generally in the various grades of our schools—it has been found to have significant bearing upon achievements in particular subjects. For all too long a time we have held a boy in grade four until he mastered what we have called his grade four arithmetic, spelling, geography, grammar, history, etc. As a matter of fact, many a boy who is a fourth-grader in grammar may be only a second-grader in arithmetic—a girl, for whom fourth grade arithmetic is an impossibility, because of her special liking for reading, may be seventh grade in her capacity in that subject. In the specific subjects, individual differences have been found to be most marked. Surely it is unfair to ask a boy "born short" in history to keep up to the pace of a comrade "born long" in that subject; so, too, it is unfair to ask a girl "born long" in geography to hold back to the pace of one "born short" in that subject. The results of these observations are leading to developments that are full of promise for the educational interests of the future.

In order that we may more fully appreciate the reality of these observations let us set down the concrete results of a few experiments.

The first three tests are quoted from Thorndike:

In a test in addition, all pupils being allowed the same time,

1	pupil	did	3	examples correctly
2	pupils	did	4	examples correctly
1	pupil	did	5	examples correctly
5	pupils	did	6	examples correctly
2	pupils	did	7	examples correctly
4	pupils	did	8	examples correctly
6	pupils	did	9	examples correctly
14	pupils	did	10	examples correctly
8	pupils	did	11	examples correctly
7	pupils	did	12	examples correctly
8	pupils	did	13	examples correctly
5	pupils	did	14	examples correctly
5	pupils	did	15	examples correctly
6	pupils	did	16	examples correctly
1	pupil	did	17	examples correctly
5	pupils	did	18	examples correctly
1	pupil	did	19	examples correctly
2	pupils	did	20	examples correctly

The rapidity of movement of ten-year-old girls, as measured by the number of crosses made in a fixed time:

6	or	7	by	1	girl
8	or	9	by	0	girl
10	or	11	by	4	girls
12	or	13	by	3	girls
14	or	15	by	21	girls

16 or 17 by 29 girls
18 or 19 by 33 girls
20 or 21 by 13 girls
22 or 23 by 15 girls
24 or 25 by 11 girls
26 or 27 by 5 girls
28 or 29 by 2 girls
30 or 31 by 5 girls
32 or 33 by 3 girls
34 or 35 by 5 girls
36 or 37 by 0 girl
38 or 49 by 4 girls
40 or 41 by 1 girl

Two papers, A and B, written by members of the same grade and class in a test in spelling:

A.	B.
greatful	gratful
elegant	eleagent
present	present
patience	paisionce
succeed	suckseed
severe	survere
accident	axadent
sometimes	sometimes
sensible	sensible
business	biusness
answer	anser
sweeping	sweping
properly	prooling
improvement	improvment
fatiguing	fegting
anxious	anxchus
appreciate	apresheating
assure	ashure
imagine	amagen
praise	prasy

In a test in spelling wherein fifty common words were dictated to a class of twenty-eight pupils, the following results were obtained:

2 spelled correctly all 50
3 spelled correctly between 45 and 48
5 spelled correctly between 40 and 45
11 spelled correctly between 30 and 40
6 spelled correctly between 20 and 30
1 spelled correctly between 15 and 20

And now the question—what has all this to do with the teaching of religion? Just this: the differences among men as found in fields already referred to, are found also in matters of religion. For one man it is easy to believe in visions and all other heavenly manifestations; for another it is next to impossible. To one man the resurrection is the one great reality; to another it is merely a matter of conjecture. One man feels certain that his prayers are heard and answered; another feels equally certain that they cannot be. One man is emotionally spiritual; another is coldly hard-headed and matter-of-fact. The point is not a question which man is right—it is rather that we ought not to attempt to reach each man in exactly the same way, nor should we expect each one to measure up to the standards of the others.

An interesting illustration of this difference in religious attitude was shown recently in connection with the funeral of a promising young man who had been taken in death just as he had fairly launched upon his life's work. In a discussion that followed the service, one good brother found consolation in the thought that the Lord needed just such a young man to help carry on a more important work among the spirits already called home. His companion in the discussion found an explanation to his satisfaction in the thought that it was providential that the young man could be taken when he was, that he thereby might be spared the probable catastrophies that might have visited him had he lived. Each man found complete solace in his own philosophy, though neither could accept the reasoning of the other.

An interesting case of difference of view came to the attention of the teacher-training class at Provo when someone asked how the lesson on Jonah could be presented so that it would appeal to adolescent boys and girls. The query was joined in by several others for whom Jonah had been a stumbling block, when Brother Sainsbury, of Vernal, startled the class by saying Jonah was his favorite story. "I would rather teach that story than any other one in the Bible," he declared, and illustrated his method so clearly that the account of Jonah took on an entirely new aspect.

Many men and women in the world are shocked at the thought that God is a personality. To them the idea that God is simply a "man made perfect," a being similar to us, but exalted to deity, is akin to blasphemy. And then to add the idea of a heavenly mother is beyond comprehension. To Latter-day Saints, on the other hand, these thoughts are the very glory of God. To them a man made perfect is the noblest conception possible. It makes of Him a reality. And the thought of Mother—Heaven without a Mother would be like home without one.

And so with all the principles and conceptions of religion, men's reactions to them are as varied as they are to all the other facts of life. Everywhere the opinions, the capacities, the attainments of men vary. The law of individual differences is one of the most universal in our experience.

Questions and Suggestions—Chapter IX

1. Just what is the meaning of the term Individual Differences?
2. Illustrate such differences in families with which you are familiar.
3. Apply the test to your ward choir.
4. Name and characterize twenty men whom you know. How do they differ?
5. Have a report brought in from your public school on the results of given tests in arithmetic, spelling, etc.
6. Have the members of your class write their opinions relative to some point of doctrine concerning which there may be some uncertainty.
7. Observe the attitude and response of each of the members of a typical Sunday School, Kindergarten, of an advanced M.I.A. class.
8. Illustrate individual differences as expressed in the religious attitudes of men you know.
9. To what extent are boys different from girls in mental capability and attitude?

Helpful References

Those listed in Chapter VII.

CHAPTER X

INDIVIDUAL DIFFERENCES AND TEACHING

Outline—Chapter X

The causes of individual differences.—Norsworthy and Whitley on the significance of parentage.—The teacher's obligation to know parents.—The influence of sex.—Environment as a factor.—Thorndike quoted.—B.H. Jacobsen on individual differences.

So far we simply have made the point that individuals differ. We are concerned in this chapter in knowing how these differences affect the teaching process. Fully to appreciate their significance we must know not only that they exist, and the degree of their variation, but also the forces that produce them. On the side of heredity, race, family, and sex, are the great modifying factors. Practically, of course, we are concerned very little as Church teachers with problems of race. We are all so nearly one in that regard that a discussion of racial differences would contribute but little to the solution of our teaching problem.

The matter of family heritage is a problem of very much more immediate concern. Someone has happily said: "Really to know a boy one must know fully his father and his mother." "Yes," says a commentator, "and he ought to know a deal about the grandfather and grandmother." The significance of parentage is made to stand out with clearness in the following paragraph from Norsworthy and Whitley, *The Psychology of Childhood*:

> "Just as good eyesight and longevity are family characteristics, so also color blindness, left-handedness, some slight peculiarity of structure such as an extra finger or toe, or the Hapsburg lip, sense defects such as deafness or blindness, tendencies to certain diseases, especially those of the nervous system,—all these run in families. Certain mental traits likewise are obviously handed down from parents to child, such as strong will, memory for faces, musical imagination, abilities in mathematics or the languages, artistic talent. In these ways and many others children resemble their parents. The same general law holds of likes and dislikes, of temperamental qualities such as quick temper, vivacity, lovableness, moodiness. In all traits, characteristics, features, powers both physical and mental and to some extent moral also, children's original nature, their stock in trade, is determined by

> their immediate ancestry. 'We inherit our parents' tempers, our parents' conscientiousness, shyness and ability, as we inherit their stature, forearm and span,' says Pearson."

The teacher who would really appreciate the feelings and responses of a boy in his class must be aware, therefore, that the boy is not merely one of a dozen type individuals—he is a product of a particular parentage, acting as he does largely because "he was born that way."

We shall point out in connection with environmental influences the importance of a teacher's knowing the home condition of his pupils; but it is important here, in passing, to emphasize the point that even though a child were never to live with its parents it could be understood by the teacher acquainted with the peculiar traits of those parents. "Born with a bent" is a proverb of such force that it cannot be ignored. To know the parental heritage of a boy is to anticipate his reaction to stimuli—is to know what approach to make to win him.

Because of the fact that in many of our organizations we are concerned with the problem of teaching boys and girls together, the question of the influence of sex is one which we must face. There are those who hold that boys and girls are so fundamentally different by nature that they ought not to be taught coeducationally. Others maintain that they are essentially alike in feeling and intellectuality, and that because of the fact that eventually they are to be mated in the great partnership of life they should be held together as much as possible during the younger years of their lives. Most authorities are agreed that boys and girls differ not so much because they are possessed of different native tendencies, but because they live differently—they follow different lines of activity, and therefore develop different interests. To quote again from Norsworthy and Whitley:

> "That men and women are different, that their natures are not the same, has long been an accepted fact. Out of this fact of difference have grown many hot discussions as to the superiority of one or the other nature as a whole. The present point of view of scientists seems well expressed by Ellis when he says, 'We may regard all such discussions as absolutely futile and foolish. If it is a question of determining the existence and significance of some particular physical sexual difference, a conclusion may not be impossible. To make any broad statement of the phenomena is to recognize that no general conclusion is possible. Now and again we come across facts which group themselves with a certain uniformity, but as we continue, we find other equally important facts which group themselves with equal uniformity in another sense. The result produces compensation.' The question of interest then is, what in nature is peculiar to the male sex and what to the female? What traits will be true of a boy, merely because he is a boy, and vice versa? This has been an extremely difficult question to answer, because of the difficulty encountered in trying to eliminate the influence of environment and training. Boys are what they are because of their original nature plus their surroundings.

Some would claim that if we could give boys and girls the same surroundings, the same social requirements, the same treatment from babyhood, there would be no difference in the resulting natures. Training undoubtedly accentuates inborn sex differences, and it is true that a reversal of training does lessen this difference; however, the weight of opinion at present is that differences in intellect and character do exist because of differences of sex, but that these have been unduly magnified. H.B. Thompson, in her investigation entitled *The Mental Traits of Sex*, finds that 'Motor ability in most of its forms is better developed in men than in women. In strength, rapidity of movement, and rate of fatigue, they have a very decided advantage, and in precision of movement a slight advantage.... The thresholds are on the whole lower in women, discriminative sensibility is on the whole better in men.... All these differences, however, are slight. As for the intellectual faculties, women are decidedly superior to men in memory, and possibly more rapid in associative thinking. Men are probably superior in ingenuity.... The data on the life of feeling indicate that there is little, if any, sexual difference in the degree of domination by emotion, and that social consciousness is more prominent in men, and religious consciousness in women.'

"Pearson, in his measurement of traits, not by objective tests but by opinions of people who know the individual, finds that boys are more athletic, noisy, self-assertive, self-conscious; less popular, duller in conscience, quicker-tempered, less sullen, a little duller intellectually and less efficient in penmanship. Heymans and Wiersma, following the same general method as Pearson, state as their general conclusions that the female is more active, more emotional, and more unselfish than the male. 'They consider women to be more impulsive, less efficient intellectually, and more fickle than men as a result of the first two differences mentioned above; to be gifted in music, acting, conversation and the invention of stories, as a result in part of the second difference; and to think well of people and to be easily reconciled to them as a result of the third.' Thorndike finds the chief differences to be that the female varies less from the average standard, is more observant of small visual details, less often color-blind, less interested in things and their mechanisms, more interested in people and their feelings, less given to pursuing, capturing and maltreating living things, and more given to nursing, comforting and relieving them than is the male. H. Ellis considers the chief differences to be the less tendency to variability, the greater affectability, and the greater primitiveness of the female mind, and the less ability shown by women in dealing with the more remote and abstract interests in life. All the authors emphasize the smallness of the differences; and after all the striking thing is not the differences

> between the sexes, but the great difference within the same sex in respect to every mental trait tested. The difference of man from man, and woman from woman, in any trait is almost as great as the differences between the sexes in that trait. Sex can be the cause, then, of only a fraction of the difference between the original nature of individuals."

It is reasonably certain, then, that a teacher may safely appeal to both boys and girls on the ground of the fundamental instincts, feeling confident that common stimuli will produce largely the same results.

Important as it is that we know what our pupils are from their parentage, it is even more important in the matter of religious instruction that we shall appreciate the force of the varieties of environment that have been operative. Though boys and girls may be essentially alike at the outset of their lives they may be thrown into such associations as to make their ideals and conduct entirely different. Fancy the contrast between the case of a girl brought up for fifteen years in a household of refinement and in a companionship of gentility, and the case of a boy who during the same years has been the pal of bullies on street corners. Surely stimuli that are to promote proper reaction in these two cases will have to be suited to the person in question.

Then, too, the teacher must realize that one child may come from a home of faith, confidence, and contentment; whereas, another may come from a home of agitation, doubt, and suspicion. One may have been taught to pray—another may have been led to disbelieve. One may have been stimulated to read over sacred books—another may have been left to peruse cheap, sensational detective stories. To succeed in reaching the hearts of a group of such boys and girls, a teacher surely ought to be aware of individual differences and ought to be fortified with a wealth of material so that the appeal may be as varied as possible. To quote from Thorndike's *Principles of Education*:

> "A teacher has to choose what is for the greatest good of the greatest number. He cannot expect to drive forty children abreast along the highroad of education." "Yet the differences in children should not blind us to their likenesses." "We need general principles and their sagacious application to individual problems."
>
> "The worst error of teachers with respect to individual differences is to neglect them, to form one set of fixed habits for dealing with all children, to teach 'the child instead of countless different living individuals.' To realize the varieties of human nature, the nature and amount of mental differences, is to be protected against many fallacies of teaching."

Our treatment of individual differences was well summed up in the following paper by B.H. Jacobsen, a member of the B.Y.U. Teacher-Training class:

The Significance of Individual Differences in Teaching

> "Individual instruction in our religious organizations as in

the public schools is under present condition impracticable. We are compelled to teach in groups or classes of somewhat varying size. Consequently, it is of prime importance for the teacher, in trying to apply that fundamental principle of pedagogy—an understanding of the being to be taught—to know first what characteristics and tendencies, whether native or acquired, are known to a large majority of the children in the class. Leaving out of consideration the possible presence of subnormal children, the language used must be clear and simple enough to be comprehended by all; the great majority of the questions must be intended for all to find answers to; the stories, illustrations, incidents, pictures, and various devices employed must be reasonably within the range of experience and comprehension of all members.

"At the same time, it is important to recognize the fact that, after all, the class as a whole does not in any very fundamental, pedagogical sense constitute the objective unit of instruction. Though it seems natural for most teachers to look upon the class as a more or less uniform mass, and the exigencies of the situation make this to some extent unavoidable, still the individual child remains always the real unit, and furthermore the units are all different—in appearance, training and temperament.

"In general the methods and material will be uniform for all, but there will still be abundant opportunity for exercising little individual touches and tricks in relation to individual pupils, especially those who vary somewhat widely from the average. Even such a superficial matter as size, especially superior size, might profitably receive a little special consideration by the teacher and thus at times save some pupil a little physical embarrassment. The boy unusually active might be given some physical task to perform, even if it has to be provided for the occasion, though it must not be too artificially created, as this is sure of detection.

"Questions requiring more than ordinary mental ability to answer may be directed to those of superior alertness and intelligence, who may also be given more difficult subjects to look up for presentation to the class. Special interests in animals, flowers, books, aeroplanes, industries, vocations, should be discovered and utilized by the watchful teacher. Even though the connection may be a little remote, any contribution of real interest and value is legitimate in order to relieve the monotony of a dull class.

"Pupils differ very widely in temperament and disposition as well as in capacity. The timid boy or girl should be given special encouragement and commendation, while the over-bold will take no injury from a mild "squelch" occasionally. The child of gloomy disposition should if anything have more smiles and sunny words sent his way than the cheerful one, who is in no danger of losing his share. The talkative child will need cautioning and careful directing, while the one who seldom speaks needs the frequent stimulus of a kind and encouraging look or word. The child who is naturally docile and obedient will develop smoothly and without great need of special attention and direction, while the stubborn, the rebellious, the untractable child, the cause of continual worry and solicitude, is the one on whom special thought must be bestowed; for his soul is no less precious in the sight of God, and the wise teacher may be the means of making him a useful citizen, as well as directing him in the way of working out his eternal salvation."

Questions and Suggestions—Chapter X

1. Discuss the relative significance of race, sex, family, and environment as factors producing individual differences.
2. Why is it essential that teachers know the parents of pupils?
3. What are the advantages of having boys and girls together in class? What are the arguments for separating them?
4. How can a teacher be governed by the force of individual differences when he has to teach a group of forty pupils?
5. Discuss the statement that teaching is both a social and an individual process.
6. Choose a subject of general interest and illustrate how it might be presented to satisfy different types of pupils.

Helpful References

Those listed in Chapter VII.

CHAPTER XI

ATTENTION

Outline—Chapter XI

Attention the mother of learning.—Gregory quoted.—The fact of attention in the Army.—What attention is.—Illustrations.—Attention and interest.—The three types of attention: Involuntary, nonvoluntary, voluntary.—How to secure attention.—Interest the great key to attention.

In that stimulating little book, *The Seven Laws of Teaching*, by Gregory, *et al*, the second law is stated in these words:

"A *learner* is one who *attends* with interest to the lesson."

Expressed as a rule of teaching, the law is made to read:

"Gain and keep the attention and interest of the pupils upon the lesson. Do not try to teach without attention."

As a matter of fact, it is impossible to teach without attention. A person may hold class—go through the formality of a class exercise—but he can *really teach* only him who *attends*. The first big, outstanding thought with reference to attention is that we should secure it, not so much in the interest of order, important as it is in that connection, but because it is the *sine qua non* of *learning*.

A boy may sit in a class in algebra for weeks, with his mind far afield on some pet scheme, or building palatial edifices in the air, but not until he *attends* does he begin to grasp the problems presented. It is literally as well as scripturally possible "to have ears and hear not." *Attention* is the mother of learning.

Think of the force of that word *attention* in the American Army. It is a delight to see the ranks straighten to that command—would that our messages of truth could challenge the same response from that vast army of seekers after truth—the boys and girls of the Church. The soldier at attention not only stands erect, nor does he merely keep silence—he is eagerly receptive—anxious to receive a message which he is to translate into action. His attitude, perhaps, is our best answer to the question, "What is attention?" Betts says, "The concentration of the mind's energy on one object of thought is attention."

As Magnusson expresses it, "Attention is the centering of consciousness on a portion of its contents." And Angell adds, "Attention is simply a name for the central and most active portion of the field of consciousness."

The mind, of course, during waking hours, is never merely passive. With its flood of ideas it is always recalling, observing, comparing, analyzing, building toward conclusions. These processes go on inevitably—go on with little concern about attention. But when we narrow the field—when we bring our mental energy to a focus on something specific and particular we then *attend*.

Betts, in his *The Mind and Its Education*, very happily illustrates the meaning of attention:

> "*Attention Measures Mental Efficiency.*—In a state of attention the mind may be likened to the rays of the sun which have been passed through a burning glass. You may let all the rays which can pass through your window pane fall hour after hour upon the paper lying on your desk, and no marked effects follow. But let the same amount of sunlight be passed through a lens and converged to a point the size of your pencil, and the paper will at once burst into flame."

To follow another analogy, attention is to the energies of the mind what the pipe line leading into the power plant is to the water in the canyon above. It directs and concentrates for the generation of power. Just as the water might run on and on to little or no purpose, so the energies of a boy or girl may be permitted to drift aimlessly toward no conviction unless the teacher wins him to an attention that rivets truth to his life.

In a discussion of attention the question of the relation of interest to attention is bound to arise. Do we attend to things because they are interesting? Or are we interested in things because we give them our attention? The two terms are so interwoven in meaning that they are frequently treated under one chapter heading. Our purpose here is not to attempt to divorce them, but rather to give them emphasis because of their significance in the teaching process.

Attention denotes a focusing of mental energy on a particular idea or object; interest, subjectively considered, is an attitude of mind. Perhaps we can get a clearer idea of the two terms if we consider the various types of attention. First of all there is what is called *Involuntary* attention. This is the type over which the mind has little or no control. A person sits reading—his attention fixed on the page in front of him—when suddenly a rock crashes through the window immediately behind him. He jumps to see what is wrong. His attention to his book is shifted to the window, not because he wills it so, but because of the suddenness and force of the stimulus. The excitation of the auditory nerve centers compels attention. The attendant feeling may be one of pleasure or of pain—there may be an interest developed or there may not. Involuntary attention clearly does not rest upon interest.

Then there is what is called *Nonvoluntary* attention. I go to a theatre and some particular musical number is featured. It grips my interest and I follow it with rapt attention, wholly without conscious effort. Unlike the case of a sudden noise, in this experience my attention is not physiologically automatic—I could control it if I chose—but I choose now to give it. Interest clearly is the motor power behind such attention. Then, finally, there is *Voluntary* attention. I sit at a table working out a problem in arithmetic. Outside there is being played a most exciting ball game. My interests are almost wholly centered in the outcome of the game, but duty bids me work out my problem. I make myself attend to it in spite of the pull of my natural interests.

And so attention is seen to be purely the result of physiological stimulus; it is seen to accompany—fairly to be born out of it—interest. It is seen to be the result of an operation of the will against the natural force of interest. This three-fold classification is of particular significance to the teacher. He may be sure that if he resorts to the use of unusual stimuli he can arrest attention, though by so doing he has no guarantee of holding it; he may feel certain of attention if he can bring before pupils objects and ideas which to them are interesting; he may so win them to the purposes of his recitation that they will give attention even though they are not interested in what may be going on for the time being. It is evident, however, that resorting to violent stimuli is dangerous, that forced attention is ultimately disagreeable and certainly not a modern commonplace in experience, that attention which attends genuine interest is the attention most generally to be sought.

One question still remains: "How shall we proceed to secure and to hold attention?"

In the first place we should remind ourselves that it is a difficult matter to give sustained attention to a single object or idea, unless the object or idea changes. The difficulty is greater with children than with adults. In the second place we should be mindful that it is poor policy either to demand attention or to beg for it.

Where attention has to be secured out of disorder we are justified in making use of stimuli that shock pupils into attention. One of the best illustrations of this sort of procedure was the method used in the David Belasco theatre in New York to get audiences quiet for the opening of the performances. Mr. Belasco was convinced that the orchestra had become a mere accompaniment to the clatter and noise of the audience and so he did not trust to that means to secure order. In fact, he discarded the orchestra idea. At the appointed hour for the curtain to rise, his theatre became suddenly dark. So dark that the blackness was startling. Immediately upon the silence that attended the shock the soft chiming of bells became audible which led the audience to strain in an attempt to catch fully the effect of the chime. At that point the curtains were drawn and the first lines of the play fell upon the ears of a perfectly quiet audience.

It is safer and better, of course, to anticipate disorder by getting the lesson under way in an interesting manner. These artificial devices are serviceable as emergency measures as well as helpful as restful variations in a class hour. Change in posture, group exercises, periods of relaxation, all help to make attention the more easily possible.

The key to sustained attention, when all is said and done, is interest. There is no substitute for the fascination of interest. As Magnusson says: "Monotony is the great enemy of attention. Interest is the attention-compelling element of instincts and desires." The teacher can feel assured of success only when he is so fully prepared that his material wins attention because of its richness and appropriateness. Special thought should be given in the preparation of a lesson to the attack to be made during the first two minutes of a recitation. A pointed, vital question, a challenging statement, a striking incident, a fascinating, appropriate story, a significant quotation—these are a few of the legitimate challenges to attention.

Questions and Suggestions—Chapter XI

1. Discuss the statement: "There is no such thing as inattention; when pupils appear inattentive, they are singly attentive to something more interesting than the lesson."
2. Explain the force of attention in the learning process.
3. What is attention?
4. Discuss and illustrate the different types of attention.
5. Give some practical suggestions on the securing of attention.
6. Point out the distinction between attention and interest.
7. Discuss the effect of monotony on attention.
8. How do children and adults differ in their powers of attention?

Helpful References

Pillsburg, *Attention*; Norsworthy and Whitley, *Psychology of Childhood*; Strayer and Norsworthy, *How to Teach*; Betts, *How to Teach Religion*; Weigle, *Talks to Sunday School Teachers*; Fitch, *The Art of Securing Attention*; Thorndike, *Principles of Teaching*; Dewey, *Interest and Effort in Education*; Brumbaugh, *The Making of a Teacher*.

CHAPTER XII

WHAT MAKES FOR INTEREST

OUTLINE—CHAPTER XII

Individual differences and interest.—What makes for interest.—Interest begets interest.—Preparation is a great guarantee.—Knowledge of the lives of boys and girls a great help.—The factors of interestingness: The Vital, The Unusual, The Uncertain, The Concrete, The Similar, The Antagonistic, The Animate.

After discussing the relation of interest to attention we still face the question: What is it that makes an interesting object, or an idea interesting? Why do we find some things naturally interesting while others are dull and commonplace? Of course, everything is not equally interesting to all people. Individual differences make clear the fact that a certain stimulus will call for a response in one particular person, quite unlike the response manifested in a person of different temperament and training. But psychologists are agreed that in spite of these differences there are certain elements of interests that are generally and fundamentally appealing to human nature. To know what it is that makes for interest is one of the prerequisites of good teaching.

But before naming these "factors of interestingness," may we not also name and discuss briefly some other essentials in the matter of creating and maintaining interest?

In the first place it is good to remember that a teacher who would have his pupils interested must himself be interested. If he would see their faces light up with the glow of enthusiasm, he must be the charged battery to generate the current. Interest begets interest. It is as contagious as whooping cough—if a class is exposed it is sure to catch it. The teacher who constantly complains of a dull class, very likely is simply facing a reaction to his own dullness or disagreeableness. "Blue Monday" isn't properly so named merely because of the drowsy pupil. The teacher inevitably sets the pace and determines the tone of his class. Many a teacher when tired, or out of patience, has concluded a recitation feeling that his pupils were about the most stupid group he has ever faced; the same teacher keyed up to enthusiasm has felt at the close of another recitation that these same pupils could not be surpassed. A student with whom the writer talked a short time ago remarked that she could always tell whether the day's class was going to be interesting under a particular teacher as soon as she caught the mood in which she entered the classroom. Half-heartedness, indifference, and unpleasantness are all negative—they neither attract nor stimulate. Interest and enthusiasm are the sunshine of the classroom—they are to the human soul what the sun's rays are to the plant.

The second great guarantee of interest is preparation. The teacher needs to have his subject matter so thoroughly in mind that, free from textbook and notes, he can reach out to a real contact with his boys and girls. If his eyes are glued to his book, he cannot hope to arouse keen interest. The eye is a great force in gripping the attention of a class or audience. They want nothing to stand between them and the speaker. Not long ago one of the most forceful and eloquent public speakers in Utah failed miserably, in addressing a thoroughly fine audience, because he was lost in the machinery of his notes. His material was excellent—his power as an orator unquestioned—yet he was bound down by a lack of preparation that cost him the mastery of his audience.

Not only does adequate preparation enable a teacher to reach out and take hold of his pupils; it makes it possible for him to capitalize on the situations that are bound to arise in class discussion. A concrete illustration to clear up a troublesome question, an appropriate incident to hit off some general truth, a happy phrase to crystallize a thought—all these things are born only of adequate preparation.

Not long ago a candidate for the presidency of the United States delighted an audience of ten thousand or more in the Salt Lake Tabernacle by his remarkable handling of questions and comments thrown at him from that vast audience. There was no hesitancy or uncertainty. He spoke "as one who knew." He was prepared. He had so lived with the questions of the day that they fairly seemed to be part of him. The interesting teacher never teaches all he knows. His reserve material inspires both interest and confidence. A class begins to lose interest in a teacher the moment they suspect that his stock in trade is running low. The mystery, "how one small head could carry all he knew," is still fascinating. Thorough preparation, moreover, minimizes the likelihood of routine, the monotony of which is always deadening. A class likes a teacher—is interested in him—when it can't anticipate just what he is going to do next and how he is going to do it.

A further aid in holding interest is to know intimately the life of the boys and girls taught. To appreciate fully their attitude—to know what sort of things in life generally appeal to them—is a very great asset to any teacher. If a teacher knows that a boy's reaction to the story of the Israelites' crossing the Red Sea is that that story is "some bunk," he is fortified in knowing how to present other subjects which are similar tests to a boy's faith and understanding. To know pupils' attitudes and mode of life is to know what sort of illustrations to use, what emphasis to put upon emotional material, what stress to lay on practical application. In short, it is to know just how to "connect up." It stimulates to a testing of values so that a teacher selects and adapts his material to the needs of the boys and girls whom he teaches.

And, finally, as a key to interest, a teacher needs to know what the "factors of interestingness" are. According to the findings of the Public Speaking Department of the University of Chicago, they are summed up in these seven terms:

The Vital
The Unusual
The Uncertain
The Concrete
The Similar
The Antagonistic
The Animate

This list becomes more and more helpful as it is pondered. It is surprising to find how experience can be explained on the score of interest by reference to these terms. Those things are vital which pertain to life—which affect existence. Dangers are always interesting. Catastrophies are fascinating. Just today all America is scanning the newspapers throughout the country to find an explanation of the Wall Street explosion. We shall not soon forget the feverish interest that gripped the people of the world during our recent world wars.

When life is at stake, interest runs high. So it does when property, liberty, and other sacred rights, so vital to life, are affected. Anything vital enough to justify the publication of an "extra" may be depended upon to grip the interest of men and women.

It is equally clear that a fascination attaches to things that are unusual. New styles attract because of this fact. Let a man oddly dressed walk along a thoroughfare—the passersby are interested immediately. A "loud" hat or necktie, or other item of apparel, attracts attention because it is out of the ordinary. Much of the interest and delight in traveling lies in this element of the new and unusual which the traveler encounters. The experiences of childhood which stand out most prominently are usually those which at the time riveted themselves to the mind through the interest of their extraordinariness.

Every reader knows the fascination of uncertainty. "How will the book turn out?" prompts many a person to turn through hundreds of pages of a novel. An accident is interesting not only because of its vital significance, but because there is always a question as to how seriously those involved may be hurt. One of the clearest illustrations of the force of the uncertain is found attending baseball games. Let the score stand at 10 to 2 in the eighth inning and the grandstands and bleachers begin to empty. Few spectators care to remain. The game is too clearly settled. As the boys say, it is "sewed up" and there is nothing uncertain to grip interest. But let the score stand 3 to 2 or 2 to 2 in the eighth and even the man scheduled home for dinner stays to the end. He wants to know how the game is "coming out."

It is easier also to be interested in concrete than in abstract things. General truths are not gripping—concrete illustrations of those truths are. If I declare that it is important to have faith, I create but little interest in an audience. But if I tell that same audience how some individual has been miraculously healed through faith, I have their interest completely. Concrete illustrations fit into and link up with our own experiences so easily and forcefully that they are particularly interesting.

So, too, with things that are similar. The mind naturally links like with like. We are fond of making comparisons. The interest in the similar is due to that fundamental law of learning that we proceed from what is known to that which is unknown and we proceed along points of similarity.

And how natural it seems to be interested in things antagonistic! Our love of contests of all sorts is evidence of the fact. Who can resist the interest that attaches to a quarrel—a fight—a clash of any kind. The best of classes will leave the best of teachers, mentally at least, to witness a dog fight. Our champion prize fighters make fortunes out of man's interest in the antagonistic.

And then, finally, we are interested in the animate. We like action. Things in motion have a peculiar fascination. Who does not watch with interest a moving locomotive? Advertising experts appreciate the appeal of the animate, as is evidenced by the great variety of moving objects that challenge our interest as we pass up and down the streets of a city and we respond to the challenge. In fact, it is natural to respond to the appeal of all of these seven terms—hence their significance in teaching.

Questions and Suggestions—Chapter XII

1. Discuss the force of individual differences in choosing material that will be interesting.
2. Why is it so essential that the teacher be interested in what he hopes to interest his pupils in?
3. Show how preparation makes for interest.
4. Why is an intimate acquaintance with the lives of pupils so essential a factor with the interesting teacher?
5. Illustrate concretely the force of each of the factors of interestingness.

Helpful References

Those listed in Chapter XI.

CHAPTER XIII

A LABORATORY LESSON IN INTEREST

Outline—Chapter XIII

Interest should be inherent in the lesson taught.—An illustration of "dragged in" interest.—Interest and the "easy" idea.—A proper interpretation of interest.—How to make the subject of *Fasting* interesting.—The various possibilities.—How to secure interest in the Atonement.—How to secure interest in the Resurrection.—How to secure interest in the story of Jonah.

"Oh, that's all right," says one. "It is easy enough to talk about interest, and it's easy to be interesting if you can choose anything you like to amuse a class. But if you have to teach them theology, and especially some of the dry lessons that are outlined for us, I don't see how we can be expected to make our work interesting."

Of course, there is some point to such an objection. Having been asked to teach the truths of the gospel of Jesus Christ, we cannot defend the practice of bringing in all kinds of material just because it is funny. And, of course, it is true, too, that some lesson outlines upon first thought do appear rather forbidding. But it is equally true that there is a path of interest through the most unpromising material, though that path does not always run alongside the teacher's highroad of ease and unconcern. A false notion of interest is that it denotes mere amusement—that it is something aside from serious and sober thought.

The writer recalls visiting a class taught by a person holding such a notion. Having given his lesson but little thought he apologized for its lack of interest by saying, "Now, boys and girls, if you will just be quiet while we go over the lesson, even though it isn't very interesting, I'll read you our next chapter of *Huckleberry Finn*." And yet the lesson, hurried over, with a little intensive study could have been made as fascinating as the reading of *Huckleberry Finn* and notably more profitable.

Another misconception relative to interest is the idea that to make a subject interesting you must so popularize it that you cheapen it. This idea is typified in the "snap" courses in school—courses made interesting at the expense of painstaking application. As a matter of fact, to cheapen a thing is ultimately to kill interest in it. Genuine interest of real worth is born of effort and devotion to a worthy objective. Far from dissipating the mind's energies, it heightens and concentrates them to the mastery of the bigger and finer things of life.

A subject to be made interesting must present some element of newness, yet must be so linked up with the experience of the learner as to be made comprehensible. It must, moreover, be made to appeal as essential and helpful in the life of the learner. The two outstanding queries of the uninterested pupil are:

What is it all about?
What's the use?

Let us, then, turn to two or three subjects which at first thought may appear more or less dull to see whether there is an approach to them that can be made interesting.

Members of the teacher-training class at Provo were asked to name four or five subjects which they regarded hard to stimulate interest in. They named the following:

Fasting.
The Fall.
The Atonement.
The Resurrection.
The Story of Jonah.

Let us suppose that I have met my Second Intermediate class of eighteen boys and girls to discuss the subject of fasting. I might begin by relating an actual experience in which through fasting and prayer on the part of the members of a particular family a little boy has just been most miraculously restored to health, after an operation for appendicitis. It was an infection case, and three doctors agreed there was no possible chance of recovery. A fourth doctor held out the possibility of one chance in a hundred. And yet a two days' fast, coupled with a faith I have seldom seen equalled, has been rewarded by the complete recovery of the boy, who is now thoroughly well and strong.

Such a concrete illustration is one possibility for arousing interest.

Or, I might proceed with a few definite, pointed questions:

"How many of you eighteen boys and girls fasted this month?"

The answers show that seven have fasted; eleven have not.

I proceed then to inquire why the eleven have failed to fast. Various explanations are offered:

"Oh, I forgot."

"We don't fast in our home."

"Father has to work all day Sunday; and so, because mother has to get breakfast for him, we all eat."

"I have a headache if I fast, so I think it is better not to."

"I don't see any use in fasting. Going around with a long, hungry face can't help anyone."

"It's easy to fast when they won't give you anything to eat."

"I like to fast just to show myself that I don't live to be eating all the time."

"I believe it's a good thing to give the body a little rest once in a while."

"I feel different when I fast—more spiritual or something."

"It must be right to fast. The Church wouldn't ask us to if it wasn't a good thing."

The definiteness of these replies, coupled with the suspense of wondering what the next answer will be, keeps up a lively interest.

A third possibility would be to call for the experiences of the pupils, or experiences which have occurred in their families, or concerning which they have read. A very rich compilation of interesting material can be collected under such a scheme.

Or, finally, I may choose to proceed immediately with a vigorous analysis and discussion of the whole problem. I arouse interest by quoting a friend who has put the query to me, "What is the use of fasting?" and then enlist the cooperation of the class in formulating a reply. Together we work out the possible justification of fasting.

The following outline may represent the line of our thought:

1. Jesus taught us to fast.
    a. His forty days in the wilderness.
    b. His injunction to his apostles.
2. Our leaders have instituted fasting in these latter days.
3. By fasting we develop a mastery over our appetites. The body is made to serve the will.
4. Physiologically, it is a good thing to fast. Many scientists are now recommending regular rests for the digestive organs.
5. Fasting makes possible an elevation of spirit.
6. Our system of fasting makes it possible to see that no one in the Church wants for food.
7. Fasting enables us to appreciate the feelings of those who are less fortunate in the world than we are, who are denied the blessings we enjoy.

Of course, each idea needs to be introduced and developed in a concrete, vigorous manner. So treated, fasting can be made a very fascinating subject.

The following suggestions on introducing the lesson on the Resurrection to little children have been drawn up by one of the most successful kindergarten teachers in the Church:

"There are several things to be considered before presenting the lesson on the Resurrection to little children.

"First, the teacher must feel that she *can* present it. In other words, she must love the story and feel the importance of it. She must also be able to see the beautiful side and remember that she is teaching, 'There is no death; but life eternal.'

"The next question to consider is: How are we going to present it? We must lead the child from the known to the unknown, through the child's own experience. Therefore we go to nature, because all nature appeals to the child. But in order to create the right atmosphere, the teacher in selecting the subject must feel that what he has selected is the very thing he wants in order to explain to the child, 'There is no death.'

"There are several ways in which the subject may be approached through nature. We may take the Autumn and let the children tell what happens to the trees, flowers, and different plants. Lead them to see the condition after the leaves are off. Then what will happen next Spring. Or we may take one specific tree or brush and talk of the twig where the leaves were in the summer, but have now fallen to the ground. The twig looks dead. But on opening the bud and removing the brown covering we find the tiny leaf inside waiting and preparing to come forth in the Spring.

"The bulb may be used in a similar way, leading the child to see the bulb as it is before planting, then to see what happens when we plant it.

"The caterpillar may also be used. Here we have the live worm getting ready to go into his cocoon and is absent for some time; then he returns, only in another form. A higher stage.

"Lead the child to see that every thing in nature has a period of changing, of apparently going away for a short time, but is not dead—it returns to life.

"Be sure to have the objects you are talking about before the class, while you are discussing the subject. If not obtainable, use a picture, or draw them."

The problem of the story of Jonah is usually submitted with a twinkle in the eye of him who raises the question. The world has so generally relegated it to the heap of the impossible that even some of our own people look rather amazed when a champion for Jonah steps forward. And yet this story properly approached is one of the teacher's greatest opportunities. If it is to be presented to small children it can be told very beautifully, either as a lesson on disobedience or, from the point of view of the people of Nineveh, as a lesson on fasting and prayer. Little children will not be troubled with doubt and disbelief unless the teacher fosters such attitudes.

To older minds, of course, the story already is a good bit of a stumbling block, and therefore needs to be given thoughtful preparation.

At the outset, with older students, we ought to lead them into the beauties of the story—beauties which all too frequently are wholly unknown to the ordinary boy or girl. Read the story:

The call that comes to Jonah.
His hesitancy.
His dodging of duty.
His selfish judgments.
His punishment.

His attitude toward the people of Nineveh.
The lesson taught.

"Yes," says the young skeptic, "but how about the whale idea? Do you expect us to believe that stuff? It's contrary to all natural law."

Let's meet the issue squarely. The Bible says that Jonah was swallowed by a big fish. Science is agreed that that part of the account is easily possible—nothing contrary to natural law so far.

"But what about the three days? That surely is."

Here is a challenge. Is it possible that life can be suspended, "and restored"? Let the scriptures testify. It was so in the case of the daughter of Jairus. (Mark 5:22-43.)

So was it in the case of Lazarus. (John 11:23-44.)

Consider the case of the Son of God Himself! Buried in the tomb, Jesus rose the third day. If you can believe in the resurrection, you can believe in the restoration of Jonah. It is interesting to note that Jesus Himself accepted the story of Jonah. See Matthew 12:40:

> "For as Jonah was three days and three nights in the whale's belly; so shall the Son of man be three days and three nights in the heart of the earth."

To doubt Jonah is to question the Master. Not only so, but if a person throws out the story of Jonah, he faces a chain of miraculous events from one end of the Bible to the other from which he will have difficulty to escape. You ask me to explain Jonah, I shall reply by asking you to explain:

The creation of man.
The flood.
The confusion of Babel.
The parting of the Red Sea.
The three Hebrews and the furnace.
Elisha and the ax.
The birth of the Savior.
His resurrection.
One-third of the account given by Matthew.
Your own birth.

May one not accept with confidence the word of God as contained in the Doctrine & Covenants, Sec. 35:8?

"For I am God, and mine arm is not shortened; and I will show miracles, signs and wonders unto all those who *believe on my name*."

Questions and Suggestions—Chapter XIII

1. Discuss the proper use of stories in securing and maintaining interest.

2. Point out the danger of bringing in foreign "funny" material.
3. Show how difficult subjects may be made of even greater interest than easy ones.
4. Use the greater part of this class hour for illustrating how to create interest in subjects ordinarily found hard to teach.

Helpful References

Those listed in Chapter XI.

CHAPTER XIV

THE MORE IMMEDIATE PROBLEMS IN TEACHING

OUTLINE—CHAPTER XIV

The steps involved in the preparation of a lesson: The aim; organization; illustration; application; questions.—Problems involved in the presentation of a lesson: The point of contact; illustration; the lesson statement.—Various possibilities.—The review: questioning; application.—The matter summarized.

So many textbooks have been written about teaching—so many points of view have been advanced—such a variety of terminology has been employed, even in the expression of a single educational notion—that beginning teachers are frequently at a loss to know just how to set about the task of teaching. Leaving for further consideration the more purely theoretical aspects of our problem, let us face the questions of most immediate concern:

HOW TO PREPARE A LESSON.

HOW TO PRESENT A LESSON.

Is there not a common-sense procedure which we can agree to as promising best results in these two fundamental steps? At the outset let us agree that preparation and presentation are inseparable aspects of but one process. Preparation consists of the work done *behind the scenes*—presentation involves the *getting over* of the results of that work to the *audience*—the class. Frequently teachers are confused because they mistake directions governing *preparation* as applying to *presentation*. For instance, one teacher proceeded to drill a class of small children on the memorizing of the aim—an abstract general truth—unmindful of the fact that the *aim* was set down for the teacher's guidance—a focus for his preparation done behind the scenes.

Though in the *preparation* of a lesson we keep the aim clearly in mind, and though, when we stand before our class, we let it function in the background of our consciousness as an objective in our procedure, we ought not to hurl it at our class. As a generalized truth it can make but little appeal to young minds, and it ought to be self-evident, at the end of a successful recitation, to mature minds.

And so with the matter of organization. We skeletonize our thoughts behind the scenes, but the skeleton is rather an unsightly specimen to exhibit before a class. The outline should be inherent in the lesson as presented, but it ought not to protrude so that the means will be mistaken for an end. Subsequent chapters will illustrate both the selection of an aim and its elaboration through suitable organization.

The successful preparation of a lesson involves at least five major steps. They are named here that the problem of preparation may be grasped as a whole. Later chapters will develop at length each step in its turn.

1. *The Aim.* A generalized statement, a kernel of truth about which all of the facts of the lesson are made to center. A lesson may be built up on a passage of scripture, on the experience of a person or a people, or on a vital question, etc. But in any case, though we are interested in the facts involved, we are interested not in the facts as an end in themselves, but rather because of the truth involved in the facts. In other words, we seek to sift out of the material offered in a lesson an essential truth which helps us in a solution of the problems of life. Attention to the aim is a guarantee against mere running over of matter of fact.

2. *Organization.* A teacher should outline his lesson so that pupils may easily follow him through the subject matter presented to the ultimate truth that lies beyond.

3. *Illustration.* Illustrations are what make truth vivid. Successful teachers owe much of their success to their ability through story or incident to drive home to the experience of pupils those fundamental truths which in their general terms make but little appeal. One of the most helpful practices for teachers who would become effective is the habit of clipping and filing available illustrative material. There is a wealth of rich, concrete matter appearing regularly in our magazines and other publications. What is good today likely will be equally good a year or two years hence when we shall face the problem of teaching again today's lesson. An alphabetic letter file may be had for a few cents in which can be filed away all sorts of helpful material. It pays to collect and save!

4. *Application.* Having selected his aim, the teacher knows the result he should like to have follow his lesson, in the lives of his pupils. He knows, too, their tendencies and their needs. In giving attention to application he is merely making a survey of the possible channel into which he can direct his pupils' activities. In considering application he asks, "Of what use will this material be in the experience of my pupils?" The test-application is the real test—both of the subject matter presented and of the effectiveness of the presentation.

5. *Questions.* Finally, lesson preparation is not complete unless the teacher has formulated a few thought-provoking questions which go to the very heart of the lesson. The question is the great challenge to the seeker after truth. It is easy to ask questions, but to propound queries that stir pupils to an intellectual awakening is a real art. Surely no preparation can be fully complete unless it involves:

The selection of an aim.
The orderly organization of material.
The collecting of rich illustrations.

The pondering of facts to their application.
The formulating of at least a few thoroughly stimulating questions.

Can we not agree to these steps as fundamental in the proper preparation of our lessons in all of our Church organizations?

With the subject matter well in mind—the work behind the scenes completed, the teacher is then prepared for the problem of presentation—is ready to appear on the stage of class activity. The first outstanding problem in lesson presentation is that of the *Point of Contact*. This is a phrase variously interpreted and often misunderstood. Perhaps it is not the happiest expression we could wish, but it is so generally used and is so significant when understood that we ought to standardize it and interpret it as it affects our Church work.

When a class assembles for recitation purposes its members present themselves with all kinds of mental attitudes and mind content. The various groups of a Mutual class may have been engaged in all sorts of activities just before entering their classroom. One group may have been discussing politics; another may have been engaged in a game of ball; a third may have been practicing as a quartette; and still a fourth may have been busy at office work. Facing such a collection of groups stands a teacher who for an hour or more has dismissed all temporal matters, and has been pondering the spiritual significance of prayer. Evidently there is a great mental chasm between them. Their coming together and thinking on common ground involves the *Point of Contact*. There must be contact if an influence for good is to be exerted. Either the teacher must succeed in bringing the boys to where he is "in thought," or he must go to "where they are."

Teachers in Bible lessons all too frequently hurry off into the Holy Land, going back some two thousand years, and leaving their pupils in Utah and in the here and the present. No wonder that pupils say of such a teacher, "We don't 'get' him." To proceed without preparing the minds of pupils for the message and discussion of the lesson is like planting seed without having first plowed and prepared the ground.

In the Bible lesson, it would be easy to bridge over from the interests of today to those of Bible days. Suppose our lesson is on Joseph who was sold into Egypt. Instead of proceeding at once with a statement as to the parentage of Joseph, etc., we might well center the interests of these various-minded boys on a current observation of today—a wonderfully fine harvest field of grain. They have all seen that. Make a striking observation relative to the grain, or put a question that will lead them to do that for you. Having raised an issue, you continue by inquiring whether or not the same conditions have prevailed elsewhere and at other times. Did they prevail in the days of Israel? The step then to the story of Joseph's dream, etc., is an easy one.

This illustration, though simple and more or less crude, indicates that to establish a point of contact, we must reach out to where the pupil now is, and lead easily and naturally to where you would have him go. Surely we cannot presume that he has already traveled the same intellectual road that we have gone over.

Suppose we face a group of adolescent boys to teach them a lesson on the importance of their attending church. If we proceed with a preachment on their duties and obligations, we are quite certain to lose their interest. Boys do not like to be preached at.

We know, however, that they are interested in automobiles. By starting out with some vital observation or question out of the automobile world, we may count on their attention. Following the discussion thus raised, we might then inquire the purpose of the garages that we find along all public highways. We could dwell upon the significance of repairs in maintaining the efficiency of cars. Now we are prepared for the query, Is it not essential that we have spiritual garages for the souls of men, garages where supplies and repairs may be had?

> The "gas" of faith.
> The "oil" of consolation.
> The "adjustment" of repentance.
> The "charging" of our spiritual batteries, etc.

Once led into the subject, boys can be made to see that spiritual problems are even more vital than material ones.

The point of contact established, we next face the matter of *Lesson Statement*. The subject matter must either be in mind already because of home preparation, or the teacher must supply it. In the smaller classes the teacher generally will have to tell in good part what he wishes to convey; in the larger classes, there are the possibilities of home preparation, topical reports, the lecture, and the socialized recitation built up by questions and discussions. It is not intended here to discuss the various methods of lesson presentation—the thought being simply that in some way the lesson statement must be presented.

Then there is the problem of connecting up the present lesson with those that have already been presented. The review is a vital factor in fixing in the mind the relative value of material covered.

Then, too, there is the matter of questioning to test knowledge and stimulate discussion, together with the weaving in of illustrative material that has already been thought out or which may suggest itself as the lesson progresses. If, as all this material has been presented, the application has been made sufficiently clear to the pupils, the presentation is complete; otherwise avenues of action should be pointed out, care being taken to stimulate rather than to moralize.

In conclusion, then, we have the matter of preparation as follows:

PREPARATION

As it involves subject matter:	*As it involves presentation:*
1. The Aim	Point of Contact
2. Organization	Lesson Statement
3. Illustration	Review
4. Application	Illustration
5. Questions	Application

Questions and Suggestions—Chapter XIV

1. Discuss the helpfulness of having a definite procedure in the matter of lesson preparation.
2. Point out the differences between lesson preparation and lesson presentation.
3. Name and discuss the essential steps in preparing a lesson.
4. To what extent would you favor adopting these steps as the fundamental processes?
5. Discuss the meaning and significance of "The Point of Contact."
6. Why is some kind of lesson statement a prerequisite to a good recitation?
7. Show how this statement may be made.
8. What do you consider your most valuable device in the preparation of a lesson?
9. Discuss the importance of filing away the material looked up in the preparation of the regular work of teaching.
10. Indicate some of the best methods of filing.

Helpful References

Betts, *How to Teach Religion*; Weigle, *Talks to Sunday School Teachers*; Thorndike, *Principles of Teaching*; Strayer and Norsworthy, *How to Teach*; Earhart, *Types of Teaching*; Betts, *Classroom Method in Management*; Bagley, *Classroom Management*.

CHAPTER XV

ORGANIZING A LESSON

OUTLINE—CHAPTER XV

A review of the steps in lesson preparation.—The values of outlining.—Objections answered.—Outlining a means, not an end.—The essentials in outlining.—An illustrative outline on prayer.

Preparing a lesson is no easy matter, particularly for those teachers who are new to the calling. There are those, of course, for whom reading an assigned chapter through constitutes a preparation, but to the successful teacher this preliminary reading is only the initial step in the process. Adequate preparation involves the following questions:

What aim shall I select out of the material available as the focus for my day's work?

How shall I build about that aim a body of facts that will establish it as a fundamental truth in life?

How shall I illustrate the truths presented so that they will strike home in the experiences of my boys and girls?

How shall I make sure that members of the class will go out from the recitation to put into practice the teachings of the day?

What questions ought I to ask to emphasize the outstanding points of my lesson?

What method of presentation can I most safely follow to make my lesson effective?

How may I discipline my class so that no disturbances will interfere with our discussions?

Reduced to simple terms, the matter of preparation together with presentation, involves the problems of

Organization
Aim
Illustration
Application

Methods of presentation
Questioning

It is difficult to single out any one factor and treat it as if it were independent of the others—teaching is a complex art with all of these factors inseparably contributing to the results desired—but, for purposes of clearness, may we not proceed to give attention to each in its turn that in the end the teaching process may the more definitely stand out in all its aspects?

For convenience, then, let us in this chapter consider the problem of organization. How to outline a lesson is one of the most fundamental considerations involved in the teaching process. In fact, it is doubtful whether there is any one more helpful attainment than the ability clearly to outline subject matter. It not only enables the teacher to proceed systematically, thereby insuring clearness and adequate treatment of a lesson, but it makes it so easy and profitable for a class to follow the discussion. Outlining to teaching is what organization is to business. Just as the aim points out the goal we seek, so the outline indicates the route we shall follow to attain the goal. Outlining is simply surveying the road before the concrete is laid.

Occasionally a teacher objects to outlining on the ground that it is too mechanical—that it destroys spontaneity and the flow of the Spirit of the Lord. It has always seemed to the writer that the Spirit of the Lord is quite as pleased to follow a straight path as it is to follow a crooked one. Outlining is not in any sense a substitute for inspiration—it is merely a guarantee, by way of preparation, that the teacher has done his part and can in good conscience ask for that spiritual aid and guidance which he then is entitled to. The fact that order is a law of heaven rather indicates that there is no divine injunction against outlining.

Of course, outlining is not an end in itself—it is a means merely to more systematic procedure. Two difficulties frequently attach to outlining: one is that the outline is made so complex that it hinders rather than helps in the matter of clearness; the other is that a teacher may become "outline bound," in which case his teaching becomes mechanical and labored. Such a teacher illustrates clearly the force of the passage, "The letter killeth, but the spirit giveth life."

But if the outline is made simple—if it is considered as merely a skeleton upon which is to be built the lesson—it is one of the greatest assets a teacher can have. Perhaps we can make the matter clearest by going through the process of outlining a lesson, indicating the essential steps involved.

Suppose we are asked to prepare a lesson on prayer. Keep in mind that in such a preparation we face the problems listed at the beginning of this chapter: the aim, the illustration, the application, etc., and keep in mind also that each of these subjects will be taken up in its turn and that for the present we are concerned primarily with the query, "How can I organize a lesson on prayer?" Let us assume, too, that we are preparing this lesson for young men and women about twenty years of age.

First of all, I must decide why I am to teach the subject of prayer. In view of the fact that the matter of the aim is to be considered fully in the succeeding chapter, suppose we agree that our purpose in this lesson shall be to establish prayer as a habit of life.

Step number one, then, is the selection of an aim—a focus for the thought of the lesson.

Step number two is the collection of random thoughts. As I begin to ponder the subject of prayer and its influence on life, all sorts of ideas crowd into my mind. Perhaps I read some one's discussion of prayer—perhaps I talk to a friend relative to it—perhaps I just ran the subject over in my mind. The thoughts that come to me may be vague and wholly disconnected. My immediate concern is content—order will come later. And so I jot down, either in my mind or on paper, such ideas as these:

> "Prayer is the soul's sincere desire."
> The Song "Sweet hour of prayer."
> What is the use of prayer?
> Are prayers answered?
> How often should I pray?
> Does the Lord hear and answer our prayers, or do we answer them ourselves?
> What kinds of prayers are there?
> How may I know how to pray?
> Should prayers always be answered affirmatively?
> What are the characteristics of a good prayer?
> What prayers have impressed me most?

And so I go on. My task in step two is to scout about intellectually in search of available, suitable material. Many of my jottings may duplicate others already set down; others may not be appropriate for my need; still others may be wholly irrelevant. But I am seeking a wealth of material that I may make my recitation as rich as possible.

Now, *step three* becomes a process of correlation and elimination—a process of hitting upon my main headings—setting up the milestones to mark my course of development. And I so sift the material in my mind and sort it out under appropriate captions. After a good bit of intellectual rummaging about, I find that my random thoughts on prayer fall rather naturally into four main divisions, each capable of expression in a question:

I. What is prayer?
II. Why should I pray?
III. How should I pray?
IV. When should I pray?

But now that I have these major headings, I still face the problems of enriching them and elaborating them so that they will have body enough to stand. In other words, I build up my sub-headings. Under the first question, for instance, I group these thoughts:

I. What Is Prayer?

1. It is communion with God.
2. It is the key to God's storehouse.
3. It is the key to God's heart.
4. It is "The soul's sincere desire."
5. It is the great anchor of faith.

Under question two, I group:

II. Why Should I Pray?

1. Because I am commanded of the Lord to pray.
2. Because through prayer I keep in tune with the Spirit of the Lord.
3. Because it is through prayer that I acknowledge the goodness of God.
4. Because through prayer I petition for needed blessings.
5. Because through prayer I establish and preserve an attitude of humility.

Under question three:

III. How Should I Pray?

1. Simply.
2. Sincerely.
3. In spirit.
4. After the pattern of His prayer.
5. In secret as well as in public.

Under question four:

IV. When Should I Pray?

1. Regularly.
2. Morning and evening.
3. To meet special needs.
4. My attitude should always be one of prayerfulness.

This matter of organization may be diagrammatically illustrated as follows:

Random Thoughts		*Organized Thoughts*
The hymn The song What is the use of prayer? Are prayers answered? How often should I pray? What are the characteristics of a good prayer, etc.?	FOCUS or AIM To establish prayer as a life habit.	I. What is Prayer? II. Why should I pray? III. How Should I Pray? IV. When Should I Pray?

In short, organizing involves the search for thought and the bringing of order out of chaos. Having selected the aim, the main headings, and the sub-headings, we now face *step four*—the enriching of these sub-headings in illustration, incident, etc., so that we may link up these thoughts with the experience of our pupils. We may think of so much stimulating material that during the ordinary class hour we can cover well only one of these questions. Our purpose and the needs of the class must determine the extent of our detail. The actual material that could be used to enrich this lesson on prayer will be given in the chapter on illustration.

Step five involves the problem of application, or "carry-over into life"—a subject to which another chapter will be devoted. Of course, we ought to say here, in passing, that application is not something added to or "tacked on" a lesson. It may be emphasized at the close of a lesson, but in reality it pervades and is inherent in the whole lesson.

Questions and Suggestions—Chapter XV

1. What is meant by calling teaching a composite process?
2. Point out the essential advantages in outlining lessons.
3. Show how outlining is not in conflict with inspiration.
4. Name the essential steps in lesson organization.
5. Choose a subject from one of the manuals now in use in one of our organizations and build up a typical lesson.

Helpful References

Those listed in Chapter XIV.

CHAPTER XVI

ILLUSTRATING AND SUPPLEMENTING A LESSON

Outline—Chapter XVI

The force of illustrations.—Three kinds of illustration material: 1. maps; 2. pictures; 3. incidents.—The force of maps and map drawing.—The appeal of good pictures.

Illustrations

Illustrative material for a lesson on prayer.

Having discussed the organization of a lesson together with the formulation of the aim, let us now turn to the problem of illustrating and supplementing a lesson. In organizing a subject for teaching we drive the nails of major thoughts—through illustration we clinch those nails so that they will be less likely to pull out of the memory.

The three chief classes of illustrative and supplementary material are:

Maps, pictures, incidents—actual, imaginary.

It is clear that in the lesson outlined on prayer, in chapter fourteen, we should have little occasion for the use of a map. We can, however, in connection with that lesson, point out the force of pictures and incidents.

Maps naturally are of greatest service in lessons with historical and geographical background. The journeyings of Israel mean so much more to us when we can follow them from place to place on a good map. So the Book of Mormon account clears up if we are similarly guided. Had we authentic maps of the lands named in the Book of Mormon, how much clearer and more interesting the history would become! We would know the exact spot on our present-day maps where Lehi and his family landed from their heaven-directed barges; we would know where to find the land Bountiful; where may now be found the ancient site of the City of Zarahemla; where flows the River Sidon; what country is indicated by the "land northward"; the journeys of the Nephites as they were being driven; what states saw there continued struggles against their inveterate enemies, the Lamanites, and how they reached their final battle-ground near the Hill Cumorah. To visit with Jesus in Palestine adds a charm to the New Testament that is really hard to evaluate, and surely the travels of our own pioneers call for the aid of a good map. Thoroughly to appreciate all that they did requires that we travel over the wonderful trail they followed—that being impossible, the next nearest approach is to see actually drawn out the magnitude of their achievement. The appeal to the eye couples so forcefully with the appeal to the ear that no classroom ought to be without its maps. Perhaps it is not beyond possibilities to conceive that at a not distant date we shall have made available films for class use to intensify the great lessons we draw from history.

Pictures make a wonderful appeal, particularly so to children. It is impossible to measure the inspirational appeal that a single masterpiece exerts on a class of boys and girls. A theological class in one of the Sunday Schools of Salt Lake County was once blessed with a most magnetic and powerful teacher. Upon his death, the class had his picture framed and hung on the front wall of the room in which he had taught. From that day to this the silent inspiration of that picture has stimulated scores of young men and women to the high ideals for which he stood.

More generally applicable and more easily available, of course, is the *Incident*. The ability to tell a story is one of the finest attainments of the teacher—particularly if he will take the pains to find vigorously wholesome and appropriate ones. May we repeat the warning that stories ought not to be told merely to fill out the hour, nor to tickle the ears of the class, but to intensify and heighten the truths contained in our lessons.

Included under the heading *Incident* may be listed short poems and all kinds of literary bits that fit in appropriately as spice to a lesson. On the subject Prayer, the following are some possibilities:

Under question I, "What is prayer?" the hymn, "Prayer Is the Soul's Sincere Desire."

> Prayer is the soul's sincere desire,
> Uttered or unexpressed;
> The motion of a hidden fire
> That trembles in the breast.
>
> Prayer is the burden of a sigh,
> The falling of a tear,
> The upward glancing of an eye,
> When none but God is near.
>
> Prayer is the simplest form of speech
> That infant lips can try;
> Prayer, the sublimest strains that reach
> The Majesty on high.
>
> Prayer is the Christian's vital breath,
> The Christian's native air;
> His watchword at the gates of death;
> He enters heav'n with prayer.
>
> Prayer is the contrite sinner's voice
> Returning from his ways,

While angels in their songs rejoice,
And cry, "Behold, he prays!"

The Saints in prayer appear as one
In word and deed and mind,
While with the Father and the Son
Their fellowship they find.

Nor prayer is made on earth alone,—
The Holy Spirit pleads,
And Jesus, on the Father's throne,
For sinners intercedes.

O thou by whom we come to God,
The Life, the Truth, the Way!
The path of prayer Thyself has trod;
Lord, teach us how to pray!

The two songs: "Sweet Hour of Prayer," "Did You Think to Pray?"

"For my soul delighteth in the song of the heart, yea, the song of the righteous is a prayer unto me, and it shall be answered with a blessing upon their heads." (Doc. & Cov., Sec. 25:12.)

The following selection:

"Prayer—sweet breath from out a joyous heart wafting gratitude to Heaven.

"Prayer—a sacred confidence between a fearful soul and God.

"Prayer—a holy balm which soothes and heals the scars in a wounded breast.

"Prayer—an angel's kiss on the longing lips of loneliness.

"Prayer—a rod that bars the way between the human soul and sin.

"Prayer—a choking sob of anguish from pain-drawn lips in plea for help."

Under question II. "Why should I pray?"

"And that thou mayest more fully keep thyself unspotted from the world, thou shalt go to the house of prayer and offer up thy sacraments upon my holy day." (Doc. & Cov., Sec. 59:9.)

"Pray always that you enter not into temptation, that you may abide the day of his coming, whether in life or in death. Even so. Amen." (Doc. & Cov., Sec. 61:39.)

"Remember that that which cometh from above is sacred, and must be spoken with care, and by constraint of the Spirit, and in this there is no condemnation, and ye receive the Spirit through prayer; wherefore, without this there remaineth condemnation."

(Doc. & Cov., Sec. 63:64.)

"The keys of the kingdom of God are committed unto man on the earth, and from thence shall the gospel roll forth unto the ends of the earth, as the stone which is cut out of the mountain without hands shall roll forth, until it has filled the whole earth;

"Yea, a voice crying—Prepare ye the way of the Lord, prepare ye the supper of the Lamb, make ready for the Bridegroom;

"Pray unto the Lord, call upon his holy name, make known his wonderful works among the people;

"Call upon the Lord, that his kingdom may go forth upon the earth, that the inhabitants thereof may receive it, and be prepared for the days to come, in the which the Son of man shall come down in heaven, clothed in the brightness of his glory, to meet the kingdom of God which is set up on the earth;

"Wherefore may the kingdom of God go forth, that the kingdom of heaven may come, that thou, O God, mayest be glorified in heaven so on earth, that thy enemies may be subdued; for thine is the honor, power and glory, for ever and ever. Amen." (Doc. & Cov., Sec. 65:2-6.)

"Watch and pray, that ye enter not into temptation: the Spirit indeed is willing, but the flesh is weak." (Matt. 26:42.)

The following incidents were related by a member of the B.Y.U. Course and are typical of scores of others available for this lesson:

Brother Hunter's Account of the Manifestation of the Successor to the Prophet Joseph

"There was a great deal of discussion among the brethren and sisters as to who should lead the Church; some thought it should be the Prophet's son; some, one of his counselors, and some the President of the Quorum of the Twelve. I was at a loss to come to any conclusion. It worried me considerably and I prayed earnestly that God would make known to me who it should be, but without avail.

"I went to the meeting that had been called and listened thoughtfully to what was said and done. The longer I listened the more mystified I became. I bowed my head in my hands and prayed for God to give me understanding. While I was in this attitude, Brother Brigham arose to speak, I suppose. I heard a voice—the Prophet's voice as natural and true as I ever heard it. I raised up quickly, fully expecting to see the Prophet, and I did. There he stood and there he spoke. I listened breathlessly. The form of the Prophet gradually changed to that of Brother Brigham, but the voice was not Brother Brigham's. It was still the Prophet's. Then beside Brother Brigham I saw the Prophet, who turned toward the speaker and smiled. My heart beat rapidly with joy and I knew beyond the shadow of a doubt that Brother Brigham was called of God to lead the Church."

Brother Huntsman's Baby Healed

"A fine, plump baby girl had come to the Huntsman home. As weeks and months passed and the child failed to use its lower limbs, a doctor was called and pronounced the trouble infantile paralysis. He said that it would never walk, for experience had showed that whenever this affliction affected the lower part of the body the medical profession could not cure it.

"The Huntsman people were faithful Latter-day Saints and did not give up hope, but called in the Elders. After a time conference was held at Shelley and Elder David O. McKay and one other of the general Church authorities were in attendance—I don't remember who. After the afternoon session the child was administered to. While sealing the anointing, Brother McKay promised the child the use of its limbs and every organ of the body.

"That night it began to move them, and the next morning stood alone by the aid of chairs. In a few days it walked, although being fairly fleshy. Soon after I moved away from Shelley, but a year or so afterwards I had occasion to go to Idaho Falls and there I met Brother and Sister Huntsman. The child was with them and ran and played as other children."

A Psychology Student Receives Aid

"A friend of mine who was a student in an eastern university told the following incident of how the Lord came to his aid.

"The psychology class while studying the relationship of the brain to life and intelligence entered into a discussion as to the nature of intelligence, and in some way the teachings of the Prophet Joseph Smith were brought into the discussion and jeered at, by all members except my friend, who was a "Mormon." His defense brought forth ridicule and intensified the discussion.

"As the class period had expired without completing the argument, a week from that day was the time set to complete it. Of course, my friend felt that he should do all possible to defend the attitude of the Church, so he studied, fasted and prayed, to secure the aid of inspiration, for he well knew that nothing but scientific proof would be accepted.

"The day came and he realized that he was illy prepared, but still hoped for divine assistance. During the giving of evidence to dispose of the existence of intelligence separate from the workings of the brain, and ridiculing the existence of a spirit, he prayed silently and earnestly.

"His turn came and he arose to speak. After the opening sentences he glanced down on the paper for his evidence and found a strange handwriting there. He says a peculiar power took possession of him. He spoke rapidly and fluently, he declared, without comprehending or at least remembering what he said. As he finished, his own writing was on the paper and he knew not what had been spoken, but there was no evidence offered to offset it.

"The professor asked him to give the names of the books from which he obtained his points, and on being told that God gave them to him, he replied, 'It's strange, but I can't believe such nonsense.'"

Under question III. "How should I pray?"

The Lord's Prayer as a pattern.

The prayer in Gethsemane.

The Bee-Keeper's prayer—1920, June number of *Young Woman's Journal.*

"And again, I command thee that thou shalt pray vocally as well as in thy heart; yea, before the world as well as in secret, in public as well as in private." (Doc. & Cov., Sec. 19:28.)

"Therefore I say unto you, What things soever ye desire, when ye pray, believe that ye receive them, and ye shall have them." (Mark 11:24.)

"At that day ye shall ask in my name: and I say unto you, that I will pray the Father for you." (John 16:26.)

Under question IV. "When should I pray?"

"He shall pray unto God, and he will be favourable unto him: and he shall see his face with joy: for he will render unto man his righteousness." (Job 33:26.)

"And now concerning the residue, let them journey and declare the world among the congregations of the wicked, inasmuch as it is given." (Doc. & Cov., Sec. 61:33.)

"Draw near unto me and I will draw near unto you: seek me diligently and ye shall find me; ask and ye shall receive; knock and it shall be opened unto you;

"Whatsoever ye ask the Father in my name it shall be given unto you, that is expedient for you." (Doc. & Cov., Sec. 88:63-64.)

"Pray always that you enter not into temptation, that you may abide the day of his coming, whether in life or in death." (Doc. & Cov., Sec. 61:39.)

"Therefore let the Church take heed and pray always, lest

they fall into temptation." (Doc. & Cov., Sec. 20:33.)

"Behold, I manifest unto you, Joseph Knight, by these words, that you must take up your cross, in the which you must pray vocally before the world as well as in secret, and in your family, and among your friends, and in all places." (Doc. & Cov., Sec. 23:6.)

"Yea, cry unto him for mercy; for he is mighty to save.

"Yea, humble yourselves, and continue in prayer unto him;

"Cry unto him when ye are in your fields; yea, over all your flocks;

"Cry unto him in your houses; yea, over all your household, both morning, mid-day and evening;

"Yea, cry unto him against the power of your enemies;

"Yea, cry unto him against the devil, who is an enemy to all righteousness.

"Cry unto him over the crops of your fields, that ye may prosper in them:

"Cry over the flocks in your fields, that they may increase.

"But this is not all; ye must pour out your souls in your closets, and your secret places, and in your wilderness;

"Yea, and when you do not cry unto the Lord, let your hearts be full, drawn out in prayer unto him continually for your welfare, and also for the welfare of those who are around you.

"And now behold, my beloved brethren, I say unto you, do not suppose that this is all; for after ye have done all these things, if ye turn away the needy, and the naked, and visit not the sick and afflicted, and impart of your substance, if ye have, to those who stand in need; I say unto you, if ye do not any of these things, behold, your prayer is vain, and availeth you nothing, and ye are as hypocrites who do deny the faith;

"Therefore, if ye do not remember to be charitable, ye are as dross, which the refiners do cast out, (it being of no worth), and is trodden underfoot of men." (Alma 34:18-29.)

Questions and Suggestions—Chapter XVI

1. Why need we illustrate general truths?
2. Discuss the value of having pupils draw up their own maps.
3. Give out of your own experience illustrations of the force of pictures.
4. Point out the value in teaching of appealing to more than one of the senses.
5. Discuss the importance of good stories in teaching.

6. What are the characteristics of a good illustrative story?
7. Take an ordinarily commonplace subject and show how to illustrate it.

Helpful References

Those listed in Chapter XIV.

Also *Pictures in Religious Education,* by Frederica Beard.

CHAPTER XVII

THE AIM

OUTLINE—CHAPTER XVII

Two illustrations of the value of an aim.—Significance of the aim in religious training.—Inadequacy of eleventh-hour preparation.—The teacher's obligation to see through facts to truths that lie beyond.

What an aim is.—Illustration.—How to determine the aim.—How to express it.

The late Jacob Riis, noted author and lecturer, used to tell a very inspirational story on the force of having something to focus attention upon. According to his story, certain men who lived just outside of Chicago, in its early history, had great difficulty walking to and from work during stormy weather, because of the almost impassably muddy conditions of the sidewalks. After trudging through mud and slush for a long time, they conceived the idea of laying a plank walk through the worst sections. And so they laid two six-inch planks side by side. The scheme helped wonderfully, except on short winter days when the men had to go to work in the darkness of early morning and return in the darkness of evening. It often was so dark that they would step off the planks, and once off they were about as muddy as if there had been no walk at all. Finally someone suggested the idea that if a lantern were hung up at each end of the walk it would then be easy to fix the eye upon the lantern and keep on the walk. The suggestion was acted upon, and thereafter the light of the lantern did hold them to the plank. Jacob Riis argued that the lantern of an ideal held aloft would similarly hold young men in life's path of righteousness.

A similar story is told of a farmer who experienced great difficulty in keeping a particular hen inside the run which he had built outside the hen house. He had put up a wire fence high enough, as he thought, to keep in the most ambitious chicken. In fact, he argued that no hen could fly over it. One hen persisted in getting out regularly, though the farmer could never discover how she did it. Finally he decided to lay for her (she laid for him regularly). To his great surprise, he watched her walk around the run carefully surveying it as she proceeded. At length she caught sight of a beam running along the top of the wire just above the gate. With her eye fixed upon it she made one mighty effort and was over.

The moral of the two stories is self-evident. Both hens and men can "go over" if they have something to aim at. It is so in life generally, and what is true of life generally is particularly true in the matter of teaching. The aim is one of the most significant features in the teaching process.

The teacher who knows where he is going can always get followers.

Important as is the aim in all educational endeavor, it is doubly so in religious training. We teach religiously not merely to build up facts or make for mental power; we teach to mold character. We should see through facts, therefore, to the fundamental truth lying behind and beyond them. Such a truth constitutes an aim in religious instruction.

One of the most regrettable facts connected with some of our teaching is that teachers leave the preparation of their lessons until the few minutes just preceding their recitation hour. They then hurry through a mass of facts, rush into class and mull over these dry husks, unable in the rush even to see the kernel of truth lying within. Little wonder pupils tire of such rations. It is the teacher's obligation to "see through" and discover the gems that really make lessons worth while.

Forty-five minutes once a week is so meagre an allotment of time for the teaching of the greatest principles of life! Surely every one of those minutes should be sacredly guarded for the consideration of vital truths. The aim, coupled with careful organization, is one of the best safeguards possible.

The aim is the great focus for a lesson's thought. It is the center about which all else revolves. It specifies what shall be included and what excluded out of the great mass of available material. A single chapter of scripture may contain truths enough for a dozen lessons, only one of which can be treated in any one recitation. The aim singles out what can be appropriately grouped under one unified discussion.

If we turn, for instance, to the ninth chapter of Matthew, we find at least eight different major incidents, each one deserving a lesson in itself. There is the case of:

The palsy.
The charge of blasphemy.
The glorifying of God by the multitude.
The calling of Matthew.
The statement that only the sick need the physician.
The case of new cloth and the old garment.
The raising of the daughter of Jairus.
The healing of the two blind men.

It is perfectly clear that all of these incidents could not be adequately considered in any one lesson. Assuming that the teacher is free to handle this ninth chapter as he pleases, we are forced to the conclusion that knowing his class, as he does, he must choose that incident or that combination of incidents which will mean most in the lives of his pupils. In other words, he centers his attention upon one major central truth—his aim. By so doing he guards against wandering and inadequacy of treatment and makes for the unified presentation of one forceful thought.

It ought to be pointed out here that every teacher must be the judge as to what constitutes for him the best aim. It is quite clear that any one teacher could find in this ninth chapter of Matthew at least four or five worthy aims. Three different teachers could possibly find as many more, each equally worthy of development. All other things being equal, that aim is best which most completely and forcefully covers the chapter or passage in question. To illustrate: Suppose we are asked to teach a lesson on the Prodigal Son. One aim that could be chosen clearly is that of *jealousy* on the part of the prodigal's brother. A second one might be repentance, as typified in the action of the prodigal. Still a third might be the compassion and forgiveness of the father, as typical of those same qualities in our heavenly Father. Which, to you, is the most forceful and significant? That one to you is *your* best aim.

The wording of the aim is a matter that gives rise to a good bit of disagreement. There are those who maintain that if the aim announces the subject as a sort of heading that is sufficient. Others contend that the aim should crystallize into axiomatic form the thought of the lesson. Of course, the real force of the aim lies in its serving as the focus of thought. The wording of it is of secondary importance. And yet it is very excellent practice to reduce to formal statement the truth to be presented. It is helpful to adopt the ruling that the aim should express both a cause and a result. Perhaps an illustration would indicate the difference between the aim stated as a mere heading, and stated fully and formally. Take the case of the daughter of Jairus already referred to,

Mere Headings:

Daughter of Jairus restored, or
The power of faith.

Formal Aim:

Implicit faith in God wins His choicest blessings.

Surely the latter is a more significant expression and offers better training to the teacher than the setting down of mere headings.

The ability thus to crystallize out of a great variety of facts a single focusing statement, coupled with the ability then to build about that statement a clearly organized amplification, is the sign of a real teacher. Instead of generalizing further, let us turn to the questions on this lesson where some laboratory exercises are set down calling for actual practice in the selection and justification of a number of aims.

Questions and Suggestions—Chapter XVII

1. What is an aim?
2. Why is it particularly essential to good religious teaching?
3. What are the objections to "eleventh-hour" preparation?
4. To what extent is a teacher handicapped in deciding upon an aim for another teacher to follow?

5. Turn to the following references and determine what possible aims might be developed under each. Is any aim adequate for the whole reference? In each case which do you consider your best aim? Why? How much of the reference would you include in a single lesson?

   John, Chapter I; Isaiah, Chapter II; III Nephi, Chapter X; Doctrine & Covenants, Section 87.

Helpful References

Colgrove, *The Teacher and the School*; Betts, *How to Teach Religion*; Driggs, *The Art of Teaching*; Strayer and Norsworthy, *How to Teach*.

CHAPTER XVIII

APPLICATION

OUTLINE—CHAPTER XVIII

The question of application.—The matter a complex one.—Various conceptions of the term as it affects the intellect, the emotions, or the will.—Application may be immediate or delayed.—How to make the application.—Illustrations.—Making the application and moralizing.—Utah moral codes as objectives behind our teaching.

Application is one of the most important subjects in the whole range of religious education. It is also one concerning which there are greater varieties of opinions than concerning almost any other subject.

What is application?

How is it made?

Is it inherent in the lesson, or is it added as a sort of supplement to the lesson?

When is it best made?

Does it always involve action?

These questions are only typical of the uncertainty that exists relative to this term.

Application really goes to the very heart of all teaching. Colloquially expressed, it raises the question in teaching, "What's the use?" Why should certain subject matter be presented to a class? How are class members better for having considered particular facts? In short, application involves the question, "What is the *carry-over* value of the lesson?"

It is impossible to dispose adequately of the matter of application in a single statement. It fairly epitomizes the whole process of teaching and therefore is so comprehensive that it calls for analysis. The ultimate purpose behind teaching, of course, as behind all life, is salvation. But salvation is not had in a day. It is not the result of a single act, nor does it grow out of particular thoughts and aspirations. Salvation is achieved as a sum total of all that we think, say, do, and *are*. Any lesson, therefore, that makes pupils better in thought, word, deed, or being, has had to that extent its application.

Application of a lesson involves, then, the making sure, on the part of the teacher, that the truths taught carry over into the life of the pupil and modify it for good. Someone has said that the application has been made when a pupil

> "Knows more,
> Feels better,
> Acts more nobly,"

as a result of the teaching done. There is a prevalent conception that application has been made in a recitation only when pupils go out from a recitation and translate the principle studied into immediate action. There are lessons where such applications can be made and, of course, they are to be commended. Particularly are they valuable in the case of young children. But surely there are other justifiable interpretations to the term application.

We need to remind ourselves that there are three distinct types of subject matter that constitute the body of our teaching material. These are, first of all, those lessons which are almost wholly intellectual. Debates are conducted by the hundreds on subjects that lead not to action but to clearer judgment. Classes study subjects by the month for the purpose of satisfying intellectual hunger. Such questions, for instance, as "Succession in the Presidency," or the "Nature of the Godhead"—questions gone into by thoroughly converted Latter-day Saints, not to bring themselves into the Church, nor to lead themselves into any other kind of action except the satisfying of their own souls as to the truth. In other words, it appears clear that there may be application on a purely intellectual level. Application upon application is made until a person builds up a structure of faith that stands upon the rock in the face of all difficulties.

A second type of lessons appeals to the emotions. They aim to make pupils *feel* better. They may or may not lead to immediate action. Ideally, of course, every worthy emotion aroused should find, if possible, suitable channels for expression. Pent up emotions may become positively harmful. The younger the pupils the more especially is this true. Practically every educator recognizes this fact and gives expression to it in language similar to the following quotation from Professor S.H. Clark:

> "Never awaken an emotion unless, at the same time, you strive to open a channel through which the emotion may pass into the realm of elevated action. If we are studying the ideals of literature, religion, etc., with our class, we have failed in the highest duty of teaching if we have not given them the ideal, if we have not given them, by means of some suggestion, the opportunity for realizing the ideal. If there is an emotion excited in our pupils through a talk on ethics or sociology, it matters not, we fail in our duty, if we do not take an occasion at once to guide that emotion so that it may express itself in elevated action."

And yet there is a question whether this insistence upon action may not be exaggerated. Abraham Lincoln witnessed an auction sale of slaves in his younger days. He did not go out immediately and issue an emancipation proclamation, and yet there are few who can doubt that that auction sale registered an application in an ideal that persisted in the mind of Lincoln through all those years preceding our great civil war.

Many a man has been saved in the hour of temptation, in his later life, by the vividness of the recollection of sacred truths taught at his mother's knee. There may be just a little danger of cheapening the process of application if it is insisted that for every ideal impressed upon the minds of pupils there must be a corresponding immediate response in daily actions of the pupils taught. May not a wonderful impression become the more wonderful as it is hallowed by the pondering of the mind through the maturing years of childhood and young manhood?

Finally there is the lesson which, though it involves both the intellect and the emotions, appeals primarily to the will and calls for action. There can be no question but that this is the type of lesson of greatest significance in religious education. We meet our pupils so infrequently, at best, that at most we can do but a fraction of what we should like to do to modify their lives. Our concern is to change for the better their attitude and conduct, and therefore we must address ourselves to the problems they face in the every-day life which they are to live between recitations. As Betts in his *How to Teach Religion* so well says:

> "In the last analysis the child does not come to us that he may learn this or that set of facts, nor that he may develop such and such a group of feelings, but that through these he may live better. The final test of our teaching, therefore, is just like this: Because of our instruction, does the child live differently here and now, as a child, in all his multiform relations in the home, the school, the church, the community, and in his own personal life? Are the lessons we teach translated continuously into better conduct, finer acts, and stronger character, as shown in the daily run of the learner's experience?
>
> "It is true that the full fruits of our teaching and of the child's learning must wait for time and experience to bring the individual to fuller development. But it is also true that it is impossible for the child to lay up a store of unused knowledge and have it remain against a later time of need in a distant future. The only knowledge that forms a vital part of our equipment is knowledge that is in active service, guiding our thoughts and decisions from day to day. Unused knowledge quickly vanishes away, leaving little more permanent impression on the life than that left on the wave when we plunge our hand into the water and take it out again. In similar way the interests, ideals, and emotions which are aroused, without at the same time affording a natural outlet for expression in deeds and conduct, soon fade away without having fulfilled the purpose for which they exist. The great thing in religious education is to find immediate and natural outlet in expression, a way for the child to use what he learns; to get the child to do those things pointed out by the lessons we teach him."

As the teacher faces this "carry-over" problem he is impressed that he must touch the lives of his pupils not only as individuals but as members of a social group. It becomes his obligation not only to direct them in matters pertaining to their own welfare, physically, intellectually, and morally, but he has a responsibility in helping to establish the standards of society to which individuals naturally subscribe more or less unconsciously.

The strong teacher's influence can be made to affect the ideals of the athletic field, of the amusement hall, of the church, of the business center, and of the home. These agencies offer such a variety of possibilities that every lesson offers easily some avenue of application. By way of illustration let us turn to a few subjects and point out some possibilities in the matter of application. May it be said here, in passing, that the secret of making application lies in not getting lost in the past so that we may walk along with our heads turned back over the shoulder of time pondering merely the things of the past. All too often the teacher hurries over into the Holy Land of some four thousand years ago, leaving a class of twentieth century boys and girls here at home to wonder what all that ancient material has to do with the problems that confront them here and now. Not that we should ignore the past. Successful application lies in reaching back into the past for a solution of today's difficulties. But the *solution* is our great concern. "We look back that we may the better go forward."

To illustrate:

A lesson on Cain and Abel may find its application in a solution of the problems of the jealousy and selfishness that exist today. This story ought not to be merely a recounting of murder. There is a little Cain—a little Abel—in all of us. Consider the case of the boy who smashed up his brother's new sled as well as his own, because he couldn't keep up in coasting. The nature of the class will determine the particular application. Or consider the story of Samson and Delilah: at first thought, a story with but little to contribute to a solution of today's problems. Yet out of that story application can be made beautifully, through either of these two truths:

> He who plays with sin will eventually be conquered by it; or,
> Marrying outside one's church is attended by grave dangers.

A lesson on helpfulness was once beautifully and rather dramatically given through the story of a rescue of a train. A lad was out at play on a railroad track when he discovered that a recent storm had washed out part of the road bed. He remembered that the through passenger train was due in a few minutes, and so rushed along the track and by frantically waving his hat succeeded in stopping the train just in time to prevent a terrible catastrophe. A few well-directed questions called for the pupils' own idea of application. They, too, would flag a train if such an occasion should arise. They could help people generally to guard against danger. They even carried the idea over into rendering any kind of service, about the home, at school, and elsewhere, as long as it was helpful.

And so illustrations could be multiplied. The important thing is that, having decided upon a central truth for a lesson, the teacher then conceives avenues whereby the truth may be carried over through action into the lives of pupils. And, of course, he must see that they are directed in setting about the action.

The question often arises, "Isn't there danger of moralizing in making an application?" or "What is the difference between an application and moralizing?" Genuine and natural application ought to be inherent in the material presented. A good story ought to drive home its message without further comment. Moralizing consists of "tacking on" some generalized exhortation relative to conduct. Moralizing is either an unnecessary and unwelcome injunction to be or to do good, or it is an apology for a lesson that in and of itself drives home no message. The school boy's definition of moralizing is helpful and suggestive:

"Moralizing is rubbing goodness in unnecessarily."

In making application of truths presented, teachers naturally face the question as to what constitutes the fundamentals in character development that are to be achieved. As a sort of guide, the two Utah codes of morals, one for children and one for youths, are rich in suggestion, both for pupil and teacher. They are submitted herewith as helpful in setting up the objectives toward which we are working:

Children's Code

I want to grow up to be wise and strong, happy and able to make others happy, to love and to be loved, and to do my part in the world's work.

During my infancy loving hands cared for me, gave me food, clothing and shelter, and protected me from harm. I am grateful for this care, and I want to be worthy of the love and confidence of my mother and father and to do all I can to make them happy.

I will be obedient to my parents and teachers; they are wiser than I and thoughtful of my welfare.

I have already learned that good health is necessary to strength and happiness, and that in order to be well and to grow strong, I must have good, wholesome food, ample exercise and sleep, and abundant pure water and fresh air—nature's free gifts to all.

My whole body I will keep clean and each part of it as sound as good care can make it.

I will have respect for all useful work, both mental and physical. I must learn to be helpful that I may know the joy of service and the dignity of work well done.

I will begin now to earn some of the things I use. I must learn how to spend, and how to be generous.

Waste is the mother of want, and even though the want may not be mine, if I am extravagant I am likely to bring suffering to others. Waste of time is as wrong as waste of things; I will not be an idler.

I will not put unnecessary burdens upon my associates by untidy, careless habits; orderly ways save my own time and things as well as those of others.

I will take thought for the comfort and welfare of our animal friends and will always avoid cruelty.

I will strive for courage to speak the truth and for strength to be fair in all my work and play, to be true to my word and faithful to my trust. I hate lying and cheating; they are signs of cowardice and greed. I will not seek pleasure or profit at the cost of my self-respect. I will be considerate of the rights and feeling of others as I would have them respect mine.

I will try to control my temper and to be cheerful, kind, and courteous in all my dealings.

I will strive to be pure in thought, speech and action.

My country has provided laws and civil officers to protect me, schools for my instruction, and many other aids to a happy, useful life. I am grateful for these benefits and will show my patriotism by obeying the laws and defending my country against evils, both within and without.

I will keep my eyes and ears open to enjoy the world about me, and my mind alert to understand and appreciate the good things mankind has provided for me—science and art, poetry and music, history and story.

May God, the kind and loving Father, help me all my life to see the right way and to follow it.

Moral Code for Youths

I am happy to be a member of that great human society which has accumulated all the treasures of civilization. I have benefited by the united labors of all mankind; for this I owe a debt of gratitude to humanity, a debt I can pay only by serving that humanity to the fullest extent of my ability. Through small services freely given toward the comfort and happiness of my associates, I may grow in power of usefulness and in my turn contribute to the welfare of the generations that are to come.

My body is the instrument of my mind and the foundation of my character. Every organ must be conserved to perform its proper function in the development and perfection of my life. I will, therefore, eat only wholesome food, breathe pure air, take ample exercise and sleep, and keep my body clean and sound. To this end, I will refrain from the use of intoxicating drinks, narcotics and stimulants; these lend only a seeming strength, but in reality they undermine my powers of service and of lasting happiness.

By abstaining from these indulgences I can, moreover, help others to abstain, and thereby increase their strength and happiness. By temperate living and plenty of exercise in the open I can preserve my health and the more easily refrain from evil thoughts and evil deeds.

I will not pollute my body or that of another by any form of self-indulgence or perverse yielding to passion. Such indulgence is a desecration of the fountains of life and an insult to the dignity of manhood and womanhood.

Through the formation of sane, health-promoting habits I can avoid having my usefulness diminished and my happiness impaired by the consequences of my own folly.

I will be modest in dress and manner, that I may in no wise encourage sensuality.

I will be thoughtful of the effects of my actions and so restrain myself that no act of mine may mar the life or detract from the happiness of my associates or of my successors.

I will deal honestly, fairly and kindly with my fellows—always mindful that their lives and their happiness are as sacred to them as mine are to me.

I will avoid impatience and ill temper and will endeavor to be courteous always.

I will try to save individuals rather than to condemn them, even though their evil deeds must be condemned and offenders punished.

I will have respect for the time of my fellows as I respect their property.

I will not engage in games of chance, since I do not desire reward at the expense of others.

In all my dealings I will strive for courage to speak the truth; I despise cowardice and lying. I will do what I know to be right, though others may ridicule or scorn me.

I will be personally responsible for all that I do, and, recognizing my limited wisdom, I will ever seek Divine Guidance to lead me in the right way.

I will strive for independence of judgment, but with due regard for the superior wisdom of my elders. I must grant to my fellows the same right of independent judgment that I claim for myself.

Whatever I undertake I will do with my might, and, win or lose, accept the result with good cheer. I would rather be worthy of success than to secure it unworthily.

I will be prompt and orderly in all my affairs, otherwise I become a hindrance to social efficiency. I will avoid waste and extravagance lest I bring needless privation and suffering to others as well as to myself.

It is my privilege to have a part in the world's work—a part I must choose and perform with all diligence. "What can I do best that society needs most?" When I have answered this question I will pursue my vocation intelligently and energetically; first, as a means of service to my fellow-men; and second, as a means of self-support and aid to those that may be dependent upon me.

May the love and appreciation I have for my country never be dishonored by any act of lawlessness or want of loyalty, but may I ever honor, uphold and obey the law and defend my country against unrighteousness, injustice and violence. When it becomes my privilege to vote I will use the right of suffrage as a patriotic means of co-operating with my fellow citizens for the promotion of social justice, peace and progress. Should I be called to public office, I will strive for moral courage to exercise authority in accord with justice and humanity; and, whether in or out of office, I will respond freely to every opportunity for public service.

I am grateful for the beauties of nature and for the great works of art, music, literature and science, it is my privilege to enjoy. These I will seek to understand and appreciate, that I may cultivate broader sympathies and fellowship with mankind, the world, and the Creator of all.

Questions and Suggestions—Chapter XVIII

1. How does application go to the very heart of teaching?
2. Discuss the various conceptions of the term.
3. Distinguish between immediate and delayed application.
4. Discuss the possibility of intellectual application.
5. How can applications best be made?
6. When can applications best be made?
7. Distinguish between making an application and moralizing.

Helpful References

Weigle, *Talks to Sunday School Teachers*; Betts, *How to Teach Religion*; Brumbaugh, *The Making of a Teacher*; Betts, *The Recitation*; Strayer and Norsworthy, *How to Teach*; Thorndike, *Principles of Teaching*; Colgrove, *The Teacher and the School*.

CHAPTER XIX

METHODS OF THE RECITATION

Outline—Chapter XIX

The question of method raised.—Danger of an entire disregard of method.—The case of the "born" teacher.—Sound pedagogy largely a matter of common sense.—Danger of being committed to a single method.—The five possible methods: The Story Method; Reading 'Round; The Special Topic; The Lecture; The Discussion.

Two of the most practical questions that a teacher ever has to solve are:

How shall I go about to prepare a lesson?

Having prepared a lesson, how shall I set about to teach it to my class?

The first of these questions has already been discussed in preceding chapters; the second now calls for our consideration.

Is there a *one best method*? If so, what is it? What steps does it involve? Instead of answering these questions directly, perhaps it will be better to point out the various methods of the recitation, set down their characteristics and relative values, and then formulate a conclusion.

At the outset it may be advisable to sound two notes of warning. One is against an entire disregard of methods. There are those persons who believe that teachers are born, not made, and that therefore a discussion of methods is useless. The born teacher, say these persons, just teaches naturally according to his own personality. To change his method would be to destroy his effectiveness. If he isn't a teacher then the study of methods will not make him one. In either case work done on methods is lost.

Of course, experience refutes both contentions. It is admittedly true that great teachers are born to their work—that some individuals just naturally impress others and stimulate them to high ideals. And yet there is no one so gifted that he cannot improve through a study of the game he is to play. Most great athletes are by nature athletic. And yet every one of them trains to perfect himself. The best athletes America sent to the Olympic games were wonderfully capable men, but they were wonderfully trained men, as well. They had studied the *methods* of their particular sports. Great singers are born with great vocal potentialities, but the greatest singers become so as the result of thorough training. *Methods* elevate them to fame. What is true of the other arts ought also to be true of teaching.

As to the class of teachers not born to the calling, it seems perfectly clear that here is the great opportunity for a study of the fundamentals underlying good teaching. Sound pedagogy is just a matter of good, common sense. Any normal person by studying how to do anything ought in the end to come to do that thing better than if he ignored it. I may not know how to operate an automobile. But if I study how to operate one, if I observe those who do know how, and if I practice operating one—surely I shall come to be more efficient as a chauffeur.

But while many will admit that this law of development applies in the mechanical world, they hold that there is something mystic about teaching for which only a pedagogical birthright is a solution. The fallacy of such a contention seems too evident to call for argument. At least the only sensibly hopeful view to take in such a Church as ours, in which so many members must perforce be called to be teachers, is that power in teaching can be developed as it can in any other field of endeavor.

The other bit of warning applies to the kind of teacher who is unalterably committed to a single method, not only as the best method, but the only one worth following. Method depends so essentially on the personality of the teacher, on the nature of the pupils taught, and on the subject matter to be presented, that it is a very dangerous thing to say that, in spite of circumstances, one method is invariably the best method.

Let us, then, turn to the different methods and consider their relative values. Five possibilities immediately suggest themselves:

1. The story method.
2. The "reading 'round" method.
3. The special topic method.
4. The lecture method.
5. The discussion method, built up through questions and answers.

1. *The Story Method.* The story is the method for childhood. "All the world loves a story." Children certainly are a part of that world. How they thrill in response to the appeal of a good story. Their little souls fairly seem to open to receive it. What an opportunity—what a sacred trust—is the teacher's as he undertakes to satisfy that soul hunger! The subject, the story, has been so fully gone into by Brother Driggs in his book, *The Art of Teaching*, that we need not attempt to discuss it fully here. Then, too, so many other excellent books have been written on the art of the story that the teacher need only be referred to them. Suffice it here to make two observations in passing. The best stories for purposes of religious instruction should possess four essential characteristics:

Point—Brevity—Message—Adaptation to the experience of pupils.

And, of course, this message should be a truth appropriate to the occasion—a message heightened by the spirit of the Gospel of Jesus Christ.

The second observation has to do with the telling of the story. Naturally it should be well told. But the story hour should not be one of mere telling. The child, in addition to listening to the story, should be given opportunity to express its reaction to the story told—should be directed in discovering the avenue through which it will carry into action the emotion aroused by the story.

2. *The "Reading 'Round" Method.* The old idea of a class coming together and sitting through a process of reading in turn from the one book in the class as it was passed about is largely a thing of the past. Let us hope that the day when neither teacher nor pupil prepared his lesson is gone forever. Surely "reading 'round" is a poor substitute for preparation. And it clearly is a dull, routine method of procedure. But there was one merit attached to it that is worthy our consideration. It did bring the scriptures into the hands of our pupils. Whatever method we may follow, this contact with the actual word of the Lord is a valuable asset. We cannot advocate resorting to the old notion of "reading 'round" as an apology for a recitation, but we can well point out the merit of seeing to it that pupils see and read the scriptures. If the lesson can be so conducted that reading is indulged in as a supplementary laboratory exercise—a turning through of gems that entice the reader to make further study of the book—then reading can be made a very valuable factor in the teaching process. Then, too, it is educational just to have members of a class turn through the scriptures to know what they are—what books are involved and where they may be found. Ignorance with respect to the scriptures is alarmingly prevalent. The following report taken from the *New York Tribune* relative to a simple test in Bible literature, given by an Eastern university to 139 students, is significant:

"Out of 139 only 12 reached 75%; 90 received less than 50%; 10 could not name a single book of the Old Testament. Some who did spelled them Salms, Joob, etc. Some named Paul, Babylonians, and Gentiles as Old Testament books."

Surely much might be said in favor of the use of books in our classes.

3. *The Special Topic Method.* Much can be said both for and against the topic method. At least three objections to its use can be raised:

A. It makes for piece-meal preparation. The lesson is partitioned off into segments, one of which may be prepared by a particular pupil who does not concern himself at all with the rest of the lesson. This method, therefore, encourages fragmentary and incomplete preparation.

B. It makes for a disconnected presentation which makes it quite impossible for pupils to get a unified conception of the whole lesson. This is doubly bad, because of the fact that frequently those who are assigned parts absent themselves from class.

C. It often results in dull, commonplace recitations. All too frequently, especially if topic assignments are the usual method of procedure, those pupils given the various topics to work up content themselves with very meagre preparation. They come to class, therefore, and merely run over so many facts wholly without inspiration and often by constant reference to notes or the text.

Of course, these difficulties can be overcome largely by the judicious use of the topic method. It ought not generally to be followed as the regular order of business, but rather as a supplementary means of enriching the lesson. It ought not to be used so as to excuse all class members from regular preparation of the lesson as a whole. If the teacher will assign the lesson proper to all of the class and then select certain aspects—certain suggested problems—for more intensive research, the reports on special topics can be made to contribute wonderfully to the richness of the class hour. The topic method, then, is primarily a supplemental method, and if wisely used has these advantages:

A. It makes for an enriched lesson. It makes possible expert opinion, and the results of special, careful investigation which the class as a whole would be unable to make.

B. It lends variety to class procedure and guarantees that the teacher will not do all the talking.

C. It fosters individual expression. It trains pupils to formulate an attack, to organize findings, and to stand and deliver a connected and well thought out message.

D. It promotes a habit of investigation—it leads pupils to work out for themselves the problems of the Gospel which they encounter.

4. *The Lecture Method.* The comment of a student of the Brigham Young University on the lecture method was unique: "The lecture method wouldn't be so bad if a teacher really lectured—he usually just talks. And talking a lot when you haven't much to say is pretty discouraging to a class."

Aimless talking which indulges in the main in vague generalities can never be justified. *Preaching* presumes a pulpit and has little place in classwork. The teacher who persists in talking most of the time overvalues his own thoughts and minimizes the ideas of others. Much talking stifles initiative and independent thinking. Then, too, it gives no opportunity for developing pupils' power of self-expression and provides no means for the teacher to check the reaction going on in the pupils' minds—assuming that one goes on! It is astonishing what erroneous notions members of a class can get from merely hearing a lesson presented. Given a chance to express their conclusions, they will themselves correct many of their false impressions.

There are occasions, however, when a lecture is extremely valuable. Frequently after several weeks of discussion a class is hungry to hear "the truth about the matter." There is then afforded a splendid opportunity for the teacher to drive home a real message. Then, too, specialists, because of their advanced study on a particular subject, can often present in an hour the results of years of investigation.

Furthermore, in a lecture, the teacher can make an emotional appeal which is practically out of the question in other methods. His enthusiasm and conviction can be made to "carry" his pupils to the contemplation of new truths. Used with discretion, the *real lecture* is a valuable asset in teaching; indulged in regularly as *mere talking* or *preaching*, the method ought certainly to be discouraged.

5. *The Discussion Method.* This method, built upon questions and their answers, is commendable for its democracy and because of the fact that it stimulates both

thought and discussion on the part of most if not all of the pupils. Questions are so vital to good teaching that Chapter XXI will be devoted to their consideration. Suffice it to say here that for all practical purposes it is the basis of the best teaching. Discussions make it possible to reach pupils "Where they are"—make it possible for everyone to contribute of his experience to everyone else.

The one outstanding difficulty with the discussion method lies in the fact that it calls for such skilful direction. It so easily runs off on tangents that the teacher is kept on his mettle holding to the subject in hand.

After all, each method has its advantages and its disadvantages. There are times when any one of them can be profitably used; it is clear that any one of them can be abused—can be made more or less monotonous. Perhaps we can wisely conclude that, *"The best method is a variety of methods."*

Questions and Suggestions—Chapter XIX

1. Why is it essential that teachers study methods of the recitation?
2. What method do you regularly follow? Why?
3. To what extent is it that a born teacher teaches without method?
4. What is pedagogy?
5. Discuss the relative value of each of the five methods listed in this chapter.
6. Discuss the statement, "The best method is a variety of methods."

Helpful References

Betts, *How to Teach Religion*; Betts, *The Recitation*; Earhart, *Types of Teaching*; Bagley, *Classroom Management*; Strayer and Norsworthy, *How to Teach.*

CHAPTER XX

REVIEW AND PREVIEW

OUTLINE—CHAPTER XX

The need of review in our Church teaching.—Review a real help to learning in that it makes for: repetition, proper connection, proper evaluation of truth.

An intelligent review is the result only of thorough preparation on the part of the teacher.—Assignment and preparation.—Ability to make assignments a test of good teaching.

Characteristics of a good assignment: It is definite.—It raises a problem.—It connects with the experience of pupils.—It stimulates to action.

General and specific assignments.—When to make assignments.

Each organization within the Church follows regularly its own course of study. At the beginning of the year it sets out upon a prescribed subject subdivided according to the number of meetings scheduled for the year's work. As a result, no one lesson stands out independent of all others, but rather fits in naturally in a sequence of chapters each of which develops some aspects of one big subject. Because of such a plan the matters of review and preview take on vital significance. Each lesson should be made to link up naturally with what has already been presented and should point out by way of anticipation what is to follow. Many educators maintain that the ability to conduct a good review and to make an effective assignment are two of the surest tests of a good teacher.

The problem of review is really one of the most fundamental processes in education. It is the great key to learning. Anyone who has enjoyed the fun of teaching young children how to read has been impressed with the fact that the child has to be led to see and repeat the simplest words over and over again before they are really mastered. It is really astonishing how many times as simple a word as "ran" has to be repeated before the beginner in reading gets it fully into his consciousness. This very difficulty of teaching mere words or letters has led to the abandonment of the old "A-B-C" drill as the first step in reading, and the substitution for it of an indirect method wherein, through the laws of association, groups of words and sentences are mastered as the symbols which express concrete and objectified ideas. But by way of experiment, one of the most impressive experiences open to teachers is to take a child of four or five that has not been taught to read and attempt to drill into its consciousness a group of half a dozen words as simple as these: cat, fan, hat, get, man, jam. To the teacher who has attempted such an experiment no argument is necessary to prove the significance of review and repetition.

Review, then, first of all, is vitally essential because it makes possible impression through repetition which insures the fixing of ideas. Literally, review means to view again. Psychologically it is to repeat the processes of mind which were called into operation the first time the stimulus in question started a mental reaction. The nervous system of man is so constituted that in the acquirement of knowledge, each time the nerve centers react to the same stimulus, the tendency so to react becomes stronger, under the mere presence of the stimulus, starts up an automatic sort of reaction, and we say that the child knows the meaning of the object constituting the stimulus.

Not only is review thus essential in the beginning of the learning process with children, but it remains a vital factor as long as men and women undertake to learn. Review guarantees recall, and recall re-establishes "nerve connections" to the permanent fixing of impressions. Very little of our knowledge remains ours to a purpose unless it is gone over and over until it is thoroughly established. A truth that is taught in a Mutual lesson on a particular Tuesday night, but which is never referred to again, and therefore never recalled, very likely will soon be gone out of consciousness and usefulness. Those truths and facts which are of greatest functioning value to us are those which we continue to run over in our minds and ponder. The reinforcement of review is what establishes our permanent working stock of truth.

Not only is review valuable as a matter of recall, but it makes for an enrichment of mental content which is altogether desirable. The real art of review lies in calling up an old truth in a new setting. Upon second perusal it is seen in skilful review from a slightly different angle so that each recall adds a reinforcement that makes for a clinching of thought which makes it permanent. It very often happens that the first time an idea is called to our attention it means but little, because our mental reaction is limited in the particular field of the presentation; the same idea in a new setting more in keeping with our experience may take on an entirely different significance. That teaching is best, therefore, which presents truth from the greatest number of angles possible, thereby guaranteeing the richest kind of associations in the minds of pupils.

Another value that attaches to the review lies in the fact that it makes possible proper connection between new material and old. It is axiomatic in teaching that pupils learn new truths and take on new experiences, in terms of the old. Teaching that unfolds—that develops new ideas that are built upon those already understood—is the kind of teaching attended by best results. In our organizations, meeting as we do only once a week, we must appreciate the fact that in the intervening time, between meetings, hundreds of ideas have crowded into the mind and have displaced those that may have been there as a result of our teaching. By calling to mind those ideas of a week ago, we not only reinforce them, but we start a chain of thought to which it will be very much easier to add the link of today's work than to proceed as if forging an entirely new chain.

No farmer goes out and plants grain on the unplowed field. He plows and harrows that the soil may be prepared not only to receive the seed, but to make generation possible.

A review simply turns over the stubble field of the preceding week's work, making ready for the planting of new seeds that they may generate and develop.

Still a further value in the matter of review lies in the fact that the review makes more easily possible the proper evaluation of the facts taught. In every lesson there are major facts and truths presented and also those minor or subordinate ones that serve to amplify and illustrate. All too frequently a class becomes so involved in the minor details that it may fail to grasp fully the big, underlying truth. By careful review, the teacher can make the essentials stand out in relief. These are the things that need to be pondered. If they are properly grasped, thanks to the laws of association, most of the minor facts will naturally attach themselves, so that truths can be retained in all of their richness of detail.

It is surprising to find how frequently pupils who have spent a year on the Book of Mormon have very little notion of the big, outstanding features of the book. They apparently have run over each week's lesson as so many independent facts, never coming back to single out the essential things in that early American civilization. Surely no class ought to complete the course without clearly comprehending such major items as:

The contribution each of the three colonies made to Book of Mormon civilization.
The general geographical location of each colony.
The outstanding characters in the book.
The coming forth of the book.
Why it is essential.
How our faith depends largely upon it.
The ministry of the Savior on this continent.
Gospel teachings of the Book of Mormon.

What is true of the study of the Book of Mormon is equally true of all other subjects. It is so easy to get lost in a maze of facts, in a course in the principles of the Gospel, and yet if a teacher will hold to such basic considerations as the articles of faith, coming back to them regularly and linking facts presented under the appropriate article, it is equally easy to complete the course with a clearly defined, skeletonized basis for all future study. Two conclusions seem obvious: as teachers we ought to conduct reviews regularly and frequently; we ought to prepare for them as one of the most vital factors in teaching.

Important as is the review, the preview or assignment is equally vital. To quote from Colgrove's *The Teacher and the School*:

> "*Importance and Value of Good Lesson Assignment.* From the foregoing consideration it is clear that no other part of the teach-

> er's work exceeds in value and importance the proper planning and assignment of the daily lessons. It is supplying the class and the school with a definite plan of work. It is preparing the mind of each individual pupil for the reception of new truths and whetting his intellectual appetite for a feast of good things. It inspires confidence by pointing out to the pupil just how he can use his past lessons and acquisitions to make new conquests. It prevents pupils from misunderstanding the lesson or approaching it with indifference or positive aversion. It enables the pupil to approach the new lesson in a perceiving mood, and helps pupils to form the habit of being successful in their work and of making a daily application of their old knowledge. It prevents the teacher from degenerating into a mere talker, and, where textbooks are used, should be the most vital part of the recitation."

The assignment is the great guarantee of a good recitation. It sets up objectives—it points the way—it starts the thought process that is to produce a discussion worth while at the subsequent meeting of the class.

Much has been said recently against the practice on the part of the teacher of saying, "Take chapter three for next time." There are superintendents of schools who refuse to keep such teachers in their service. To make such an assignment, particularly in classes that meet only once a week, and especially if the assignment is made, as is too usually the case, after the signal for class dismissal has been given, is to promise the pupils a week in advance that their next lesson will be very much of a failure.

A good assignment is characterized by several very definite features. In the first place it is perfectly clear. Given at a time when pupils are following it, it gives specific direction as to the work to be done ahead in preparation. It indicates the direction of intellectual travel, points out sources of material, and indicates what is to be looked for. Reference or textbooks are so pointedly referred to that pupils not only remember their names, they want to turn to them to enjoy their contributions.

In the second place, a good assignment raises a problem which is a challenge to the mental powers of pupils. It should carry a force of anticipation that capitalizes on that great mover to action—curiosity. For instance, if the lesson to be assigned is one on baptism, instead of simply naming certain pages in a text to be read, the skilful teacher may well challenge his class by bringing in a clipping from a periodical or from some other source attempting to prove that sprinkling is the correct method of baptism, or that baptism is not essential to a man's obtaining salvation? How can members of the class meet such an argument? One of their first thoughts will likely be a query as to where available material may be turned to. How easy, then, to give references, etc. Some such problem can be raised relative to every lesson taught, and it is a wonderful force as an intellectual appetizer. It should both prompt to action and point to the path to be followed.

The question is often raised as to whether the assignment should be general or specific. Perhaps the best answer involves both kinds. There ought ordinarily to be a general assignment that affects all of the members of a class. The class is made up of all the individuals in the group—its discussing ought therefore to be so made up. But in addition to this general assignment, specific topics given to particular members add an enrichment to the recitation of very great value. The services of the specialist are always of inestimable value. That class is best wherein each member in turn becomes a specialist in looking up and bringing in vital observations on life.

As to the best time for making assignments, it is rather hard to give a ruling that best fits all cases. Preferably the assignment should grow out of the discussion of the lesson in hand, and therefore logically comes at the end of the recitation rather than at the beginning. There are teachers, however, who, fearing interruption at the end of the hour, map out their work so carefully that they can make the assignment at the outset, merely calling attention to it at the close of the hour. All other things being equal, if the teacher will make himself hold sacred the time necessary at the end of the hour for this all important matter of assignment, it is likely that best results will follow having the assignment of the next lesson grow naturally out of the work of today. The important thing, however, is that at some point in the recitation, the teacher shall take plenty of time to make a carefully planned and challenging announcement of the work ahead.

Questions and Suggestions—Chapter XX

1. Why is it essential to good teaching that regular reviews be conducted?
2. Why are reviews more necessary in our religious work than in regular school work?
3. What are the chief purposes of a review?
4. By taking a current lesson of one of the auxiliary organizations, illustrate the work done in a good review.
5. Why it is of vital importance that a teacher give special preparation to a review?
6. Show how good class preparation is conditional upon the proper kind of assignment.
7. What are the characteristics of a good assignment?
8. What is the best time for making the assignment?
9. Show how to make a good assignment of a current lesson from one of the organizations.

Helpful References

Betts, *The Recitation*; Betts, *How to Teach Religion*; Colvin, *The Learning Process*; Colgrove, *The Teacher and the School*; Strayer and Norsworthy, *How to Teach.*

CHAPTER XXI

THE QUESTION AS A FACTOR IN EDUCATION

Outline—Chapter XXI

Taking Stock.—Miss Stevens' study on questioning.—Miss Stevens quoted.—Various types of questions: a. The review question; b. The fact question; c. The leading question; d. The thought or challenging question.—Some questions on questioning.

How many questions do you ask regularly during a recitation?

What proportion of those questions are answered in full and complete statements?

How many of the answers to your questions are a matter merely of memory? How many reveal original, creative thinking?

Such questions as these not only impress us with the force of the question as a means of teaching, but they lead us to examine into our own method of asking them. The whole teaching process so easily and unconsciously develops into a matter of routine that it is good practice occasionally to take stock of ourselves. It is surprising to find how many teachers develop a particular type of question which becomes their sole stock in trade.

Miss Ronniett Stevens, in her thesis, *The Question as a Measure of Efficiency in Instruction*, has made one of the most enlightening studies yet made on the matter of questioning. Her results are quoted by Weigle, in his *Talks to Sunday School Teachers*, in a passage of interest, not only because of Miss Stevens' findings, but also because of Mr. Weigle's own conclusions:

> "One of the outstanding differences, in present practice, between the public and the Sunday school, is that most public school teachers ask too many questions and most Sunday school teachers do not ask questions enough. For the first half of this statement there is ample evidence in the careful study by Miss Ronniett Stevens on *The Question as a Measure of Efficiency in Instruction*. Miss Stevens secured complete stenographic reports of twenty high school lessons in English, history, science, Latin, modern languages, and mathematics; she observed one hundred more such lessons chosen at random, with a view to counting and noting the number and nature of the questions asked in each; and

she followed each ten classes through an entire day's work for the purpose of studying the aggregate question-stimulus to which each was subjected in the course of the day.

"The results of her study are surprising. In only eight of the twenty lessons completely reported the teacher asked less than ninety questions in the period of forty-five minutes, the average being sixty-eight. In each of the remaining twelve lessons more than ninety questions were asked in the same period of time, the average being 128. A freshman class in high school, in a day's work of five periods of forty minutes each, not counting gymnasium, was subjected to 516 questions and expected to return 516 answers, which is at the rate of 2:58 questions and 2:58 answers per minute. The lowest number of questions recorded in a day's work for a class was 321, and the average number 395.

"Such rapid-fire questioning, Miss Stevens rightly holds, defeats its own ends. It maintains a nervous tension in the classroom that must in the long run be injurious. More than that, it is a symptom of the fact that the real work of the hour is being done by the teacher, and the pupil's share is reduced simply to brief, punctuation-like answers to the teacher's questions. Such questions appeal to mere memory or to superficial judgment rather than to real thought; they cultivate in the pupil neither independent judgment nor the power of expression; they ignore individual needs and discourage initiative; they make out of the classroom a place to display knowledge, rather than a laboratory in which to acquire it.

"The second half of the proposition, that most Sunday school teachers do not ask questions enough, has not been established by any such investigation as that of Miss Stevens. A similar study, on the basis of complete stenographic reports, of typical Sunday school lessons, would be a most valuable addition to our resources in the field of religious pedagogy. Till such a study is made, one must simply record his conviction that Sunday school teachers, as a general rule, ask too few, rather than too many questions. This conviction is based upon general observation and upon the frequency of such remarks as, 'I just can't get my class to study,' 'There are only two or three who ever answer my questions,' 'My pupils don't know anything about the Bible,' 'As long as I do all the talking, things go all right,' etc." Weigle, *Talks to Sunday School Teachers*.

The whole matter of questioning can be made to stand out most clearly, perhaps, by listing the various types of question, the purposes which each type serves, and the characteristics of a good question.

First of all there is the *Review question*. The great purpose of this type of question is to systematize knowledge. Of course, it is valuable as an aid to recollection—it is a challenge to memory—but it is particularly helpful in that it makes the big essential points in a course stand out in relief with minor points properly correlated and subordinated. The review question is a guide to the pupil whereby he may see the relative significance of the work he has covered. One of our great difficulties lies in the fact that our teaching is so largely piece-meal. Today's lesson is hurried through, isolated as it is from all that has gone before and all that may follow. The successful teacher through the review makes each lesson a link in the chain of thought that underlies the whole development of the subject in hand.

The review question is essentially a carefully thought out, searching inquiry. It calls for a turning over, in the mind, of the material of the whole course and therefore should allow ample time for pondering. If it does not stimulate a "weighing process," it likely is merely a fact question—a test of memory. Of course, there is a place at times for this hurried type of question, but it serves the purpose only of "connecting up" and should not be mistaken for the evaluating question of review.

The following questions on the expulsion of the Saints from Missouri are illustrative review questions:

1. To what extent, if any, were the Latter-day Saints themselves responsible for their expulsion from Missouri?
2. To what extent were the persecutions of Missouri political? Religious?
3. How do you account for the fact that the Lord's people have always been a chastened people?
4. Show how the Missouri persecutions have been ultimately a blessing to the Latter-day Saints.

The second type of question is the *fact* question. It serves to check up on mental alertness and recall. It is often helpful in arresting attention and therefore has a certain disciplinary function. The teacher, of course, must make sure that his pupils are grasping the subject-matter presented, and the fact question serves admirably as a test of knowledge. It is usually a short question calling for a short answer, and therefore may be used in a rapid-fire way that stimulates thought. It is this type of question that is hurled so frequently at classes with the consequences pointed out in the quotation from Miss Stevens.

The same author lists as objections to the continued use of these rapid-fire questions the following bad features. They result in:

1. Nervous tension.
2. The teacher's doing most of the work.
3. Emphasis upon memory and superficial judgment.
4. Little time for the art of expression.
5. Little attention to the needs of particular individuals in a class.
6. The class being made a place for displaying knowledge.
7. Little self-reliant, independent thinking.

As illustrative of the fact question may we set down the following:

Who was Joseph Smith?
What was his father's name?
What was his mother's name?
Where was he born?
How old was he when he received his first vision?
When did he receive the plates?

The *challenging question* and the *leading question* are closely enough allied that we may well discuss them together. They are both intended to provoke creative thinking. The leading question aims to capitalize on what is already in the pupil's mind in getting him to go one step further to a conclusion we already have in mind. Instead of telling a class of young children that Joseph Smith prayed to the Lord for help in choosing the church to which he might best belong, we might proceed by saying that the Prophet had asked his father and mother—he had asked his best friends—he had talked with all the ministers he could find—he had read in all of the available books—now who can tell what else he could do? The chief merit of the leading question lies in the fact that it paves the way for the answer. It is particularly helpful in encouraging young and backward pupils. But is easily subject to abuse. So much so that its use is very largely restricted in law courts. It results too frequently in the teacher's thinking for the pupil, and therefore ought to be used with care.

The challenging question is the question that fosters originality of thought, independence of judgment. It simply raises a problem and leaves pupils free to arrive at their own conclusions. It makes for an intelligent faith so much desired in a democratic Church such as ours. It is the one question above all others that guarantees a vital class distinction.

Of course, there is a place for all four of these types of questions. As was said relative to the methods of the recitation, the best method is a variety of methods. So with questions. It is perfectly clear, however, that for general purposes that question which prompts greatest reflection and independent thinking is the best one to indulge most frequently. The following questions out of a lesson on Joseph Smith's First Vision are set down as typical of thought-provoking questions:

1. In view of the fact that when men choose a man for president of a bank they look for a man of maturity and experience, how do you explain that Joseph Smith, a mere boy, with little training or experience, was entrusted with the great responsibility of founding what we claim is the greatest institution of these latter days?

2. How can you convince the world that a just God would declare that none of their churches is right?

3. What vital truths are announced to the world through his first vision?

Let us conclude this chapter with one more quotation from Miss Stevens. When asked to name the three outstanding characteristics of a good question, she set them down as follows:

1. A good question should stimulate reflection.
2. It should be adapted to the experience of the pupil.
3. It should draw forth a well-rounded answer.

Questions on Questioning

Do I call on my pupils to recite in a fixed order, according to alphabet or seating, so that they are warned not to attend till their turn comes?

Do I name the pupil who is to answer before I put the question?

Do I ask direct questions or alternative questions which can be answered without knowledge or thought?

Do I ask chiefly fact questions?

Do I ask leading or suggestive questions?

Do I repeat my questions? Attention.

Do I answer my own questions?

Do I ask confusing, changed questions?

Do I ask foolish questions that no one can answer?

Do my questions make pupils think?

Do my questions follow up the answer and lead to new organization of knowledge?

Do I repeat the pupil's answer?

Do my questions reach all the members of the class?

Do I make the recitation an inquisition, or do I pursue a slow pupil and listen while pupils express themselves freely and naturally?

Questions and Suggestions—Chapter XXI

1. Why is it essential that we prepare questions as we do other material?
2. What are the dangers that attend the asking of a great number of fact questions?
3. Discuss the relative value of the "W's"—what, who, when, where, and why.
4. Discuss each of the questions on questioning in this chapter.
5. Bring in three thought-provoking questions on one of the current lessons in the month's work of one of the auxiliary organizations.

Helpful References

Fitch, *The Art of Questioning*; Stevens, *The Question as a Measure of Efficiency in Instruction*; Weigle, *Talks to Sunday School Teachers*; Horne, *Story Telling, Questioning, and Studying*; Brumbaugh, *The Making of a Teacher*; Driggs, *The Art of Teaching*.

CHAPTER XXII

THE PROBLEM OF DISCIPLINE

OUTLINE—CHAPTER XXII

A popular misconception of discipline.—Discipline inherent in teaching.—Importance of discipline in our religious teaching.—Changed attitude within the past three centuries toward discipline.—What discipline is.

Methods of securing discipline: The method of rewards; The method of "pleasing the teacher"; The method of punishment; The method of social appeal; The method of interest.

The importance of a proper attitude on the part of one who disciplines.—What constitutes such an attitude?

Back in 1916 the writer of these chapters was invited to address a group of teachers on the subject of discipline. This particular lecture came toward the end of a series of lectures given on the various pedagogical truths underlying teaching. One particular teacher, who had listened to all of the lectures, expressed appreciation of the fact that discipline was to be discussed—it apparently was his one concern, as indicated in his remark:

"We have listened to some excellent theories in these lectures. But I have to teach a class of real live boys and girls. How can I keep the little rascals quiet long enough to work the theories out?"

The remark expresses admirably the attitude of very many teachers relative to discipline. They regard teaching as one thing—discipline as quite another. With them discipline involves some sort of magic process or the application of some iron rule authority, which secures order that teaching may then be indulged in. As a matter of fact, discipline is inherent in good teaching. It is not a matter of correction so much as a matter of prevention. The good disciplinarian anticipates disorder—directs the energies of his pupils so that the disorder is made impossible by attention to legitimate interests.

Discipline is one of the most pressing problems in the quorums and organizations of the Church today. On every hand the complaint is registered that proper respect is not shown, either for those in important positions or for our places of worship.

The spirit that accompanies the political rally or basketball game, held in our amusement halls, too frequently is carried into our sacred meetings. The spirit of unconcern is carried into our classrooms until all too often to call the condition one of disorder is a very inadequate description of the procedure.

It is interesting to note the changing attitude generally in the matter of discipline. The harshness of other days is largely replaced by a leniency that borders on "easiness." Our whole attitude toward criminals has been revolutionized, and our human impulses have carried over into the realm of teaching, until now, at least in the opinion of very many critics, we have drifted largely into "soft pedagogy"—a process of trying to please regardless of the consequences.

Earlier treatises on education devoted a good bit of space to the amount and kind of punishment that should be administered in a well-ordered school. Punishment is decidedly out of taste these days. The biography of an old German master discloses the fact that during his teaching career he had administered 911,527 raps with his cane, 20,989 with a ruler, 136,715 with his hand, and that he was responsible for 1,115,800 slaps on the head. The same attitude is reflected in the fact that in England, as late as the year 1800, two hundred twenty-three offenses were punishable by death. The offenses included shooting rabbits, stealing, defacing Westminster Bridge, etc. In our day we hesitate to apply the extreme penalty even to the murderer.

The attitude toward the content of teaching has undergone a change quite in keeping with that attached to method. There was a time when pedagogical philosophy rather hinted, "It doesn't make any difference what you teach a boy, as long as he doesn't like it." The hint these days might more nearly read: "It doesn't make any difference how valuable certain material is for a boy, don't attempt to teach it to him unless it fascinates him." Our effort to interest our pupils has practically resulted in taking the scriptures, particularly the Old Testament, out of our organizations. Of course, the doctrine of interest is a very vital one, but there are bounds beyond which we ought not to push it.

It is, therefore, perfectly obvious that there is urgent need of discipline. Any effort at social control demands it. The army succeeds as it does because of its discipline. Wherever a group of individuals undertake action in common, every member must be willing to sink *interests* of *self* in *welfare* of *others*. As was pointed out in the chapter on Individual Differences, a class is made up of all kinds of individuals. They vary in capacity, in ideals, in training, in attitude, in disposition, and in purpose. Manifestly group progress will be made possible in any such case by a mutual willingness to co-operate—a willingness to attend a discussion even though not particularly interested in it, but because it may be of concern to someone else whose interests I have undertaken to promote. My very presence in the class imposes such a responsibility upon me.

It is essential in a discussion of discipline that we agree as to just what discipline is. It is not *mere silence*. Silent "quietness" may be agreeable, but it certainly does not make for achievement. Such silence would be of little worth if it could be achieved, and it cannot be achieved with twentieth century human beings. The question of the lad who had been taken to task for his disturbance is always refreshing. The teacher, after a somewhat prolonged scolding, had concluded:

"Now, Tommie, do be quiet."

"What fur?"

The English may not be the choicest, but the sense is wonderfully significant to the teacher who would really understand the problem of discipline.

Discipline is not repression. The *D* of discipline and the *D* of don't have been confused all too often. Just as the too frequent use of the brakes on an automobile ruins the lining, so the too frequent "don't" of repression ruins the "goodwill lining" of the boy, and when that lining is gone the "brake squeaks," and in emergencies doesn't hold at all.

Discipline rather consists in that direction of wholesome activity which creates an atmosphere of intellectual endeavor in which every individual of a group can profitably follow his own interests while allowing every other individual to do the same thing free from interference. Discipline makes it possible for all to do the thing to be done to advantage. It may at times require silence, it may involve vigorous action—it always presumes intelligent direction that holds those concerned to the orderly pursuit of an established goal.

Various means have been devised for the securing of discipline. The *doctrine of rewards* has been and still is being followed extensively. To give an individual something for being good has never appealed to educators as fundamentally sound. It puts a false evaluation upon virtue. It may be that such a policy must be resorted to in emergencies, but followed regularly it is likely to be attended with disastrous results. The boy who has regularly to be bought into doing what he should will likely raise his price until the method of rewards becomes ruinous both to the father and the boy. To "heroize" a boy in class every time he does a meritorious act will very likely spoil him. Encouragement, of course, is helpful, but it ought not to be overindulged. A stick of candy may induce a child to go to bed agreeably each night, but the candy may spoil other things than the bedspread. Moral fibre is built up by developing the habit of doing a thing because it is right—because it ought to be done. There are teachers and preachers who hold the interest of those taught by tickling their ears with material, either funny or nonsensical. There is a question whether it is not a dangerous practice in an effort to win them to what should be an attitude of religious devotion.

Then there is the doctrine that children should be good to please their parents and teachers. This doctrine is akin to that of rewards. It sets up something of a false ideal, though of course it is a splendid thing to teach appreciation of those who help us. Much can be defended which seeks to inculcate in the minds of children reverence for their elders. The chief difficulty lies in the fact that this doctrine may not continue to appeal as fundamentally sound.

A third method for securing discipline is to compel it. This is to resort to the law of things. A certain amount of law should characterize both the home and the classroom. Obedience and order are the first laws of heaven and are essential to good social environment. But the law should be so administered that the obedience exacted rests upon an intelligent understanding of the purpose behind the law. Otherwise there comes a time when mere authority fails to control. It is a good thing to train children to abide by regulations out of a sense of duty. If duty and love can be coupled, the combination makes for permanent law-abiding. Arbitrary authority and blind obedience have produced Germany. Strong leadership coupled with democratic co-operation and loyalty have produced America.

Still another doctrine of discipline rests upon a social appeal. Members of a group agree that in the interest of everyone's welfare each individual will subscribe to certain conditions regardless of their application to him. This principle, fundamental in all democracies, can safely be trusted to secure desired results in groups mature enough to assure sound judgment. The sense of justice in the human soul is a safe guarantee of both liberty and good order. Many of our classes no doubt could be improved noticeably if we could enlist the co-operation of the members to the extent that they would assume to govern themselves.

Finally there is the doctrine of interest as a means of maintaining discipline. This doctrine implies that a teacher should get his class so interested in doing what he wants it to do that it hasn't any inclination to do what it ought not to do. This doctrine is not the pernicious doctrine hinted at earlier in this chapter of cheapening everything into "easiness." Genuine interest may lead not only to effort, but to sacrifice. The boy who plays football does not play because of the ease of the game—he is fascinated by his interest in the struggle. Ample preparation and a complete understanding of pupils will make possible an interest that disciplines without any evidence of discipline. Surely this is the modern doctrine of discipline, though with it should be coupled that wholesome respect for authority that prompts citizens to abide by the law.

No discussion of discipline would be complete which did not mention at least the significance of attitude on the part of one who disciplines. In so many cases when a boy is corrected he complains of the teacher,

"Oh, well, he's got it in for me."

It is always interesting to know whether a parent or teacher disciplines a child because the child needs it, or because the parent or teacher is unnerved and has to give expression to his feelings. The disciplinarian who can correct, when correction is necessary, both in firmness yet in fairness, so that the person who is corrected is made to feel that the correction grows out of a desire to help rather than merely to punish—that disciplinarian will exert an influence for good that is hard to estimate. He is both a friend and a benefactor.

Let us conclude this chapter with that wonderful passage from the Doctrine & Covenants which gives us the word of the Lord on this matter of controlling others:

> "Behold, there are many called, but few are chosen. And why are they not chosen?
>
> "Because their hearts are set so much upon the things of this world, and aspire to the honors of men, that they do not learn this

one lesson—

"That the rights of the Priesthood are inseparably connected with the powers of heaven, and that the powers of heaven cannot be controlled nor handled only upon the principles of righteousness.

"That they may be conferred upon us, it is true; but when we undertake to cover our sins, or to gratify our pride, our vain ambitions, or to exercise control, or dominion, or compulsion, upon the souls of the children of men, in any degree of unrighteousness, behold, the heavens withdraw themselves; the Spirit of the Lord is grieved; and when it is withdrawn, Amen to the Priesthood, or the authority of that man.

"Behold! ere he is aware, he is left unto himself, to kick against the pricks; to persecute the Saints, and to fight against God.

"We have learned, by sad experience, that it is the nature and disposition of almost all men, as soon as they get a little authority, as they suppose, they will immediately begin to exercise unrighteous dominion.

"Hence many are called, but few are chosen.

"No power or influence can or ought to be maintained by virtue of the Priesthood, only by persuasion, by long suffering, by gentleness, and meekness, and by love unfeigned;

"By kindness, and pure knowledge, which shall greatly enlarge the soul without hypocrisy, and without guile;

"Reproving betimes with sharpness, when moved upon by the Holy Ghost, and then showing forth afterwards an increase of love toward him whom thou hast reproved, lest he esteem thee to be his enemy;

"That he may know that thy faithfulness is stronger than the cords of death;

"Let thy bowels also be full of charity towards all men, and to the household of faith, and let virtue garnish thy thoughts unceasingly, then shall thy confidence wax strong in the presence of God, and the doctrine of the Priesthood shall distil upon thy soul as the dews from heaven.

"The Holy Ghost shall be thy constant companion, and thy sceptre an unchanging sceptre of righteousness and truth, and thy dominion shall be an everlasting dominion, and without compulsory means it shall flow unto thee forever and ever." (Doc. & Cov., Sec. 121:34-46.)

Questions and Suggestions—Chapter XXII

1. What constitutes good discipline?
2. What factors contribute to make discipline a real problem in our Church?
3. Discuss our attitude toward discipline today as compared with the attitude toward it a generation ago.
4. Name the various methods of securing discipline.
5. Discuss their relative values.
6. Why is the teacher's attitude so important a factor in discipline?
7. What qualities are involved in the proper attitude?
8. Discuss preparation in its bearing upon discipline.

Helpful References

Doctrine & Covenants; Bagley, *School Discipline*; O'Shea, *Everyday Problems in Teaching*; Brumbaugh, *The Making of a Teacher*; Dewey, *Interest and Effort in Education.*

CHAPTER XXIII

CREATING CLASS SPIRIT

Outline—Chapter XXIII

The "pull" of a good class.—The appeal of an attractive classroom.—Making it "our room."—The teacher and class spirit.—Capitalizing on the leadership of the class.—Stimulating free participation.—Out of class activities.—Some possibilities.

There is a "pull" to certain classes—a pull that has all the force of a magnet. Pupils not only go to such a class willingly, but anticipate with pleasure the approach of the recitation hour. When duty is coupled with pleasure, there is a force for righteousness that is beyond measure. Of the various factors that contribute to the creation of a class spirit, the following are offered as being among the most helpful.

1. *An Attractive Classroom.* While it is true that most of the organizations in the Church do not have surplus funds for beautifying their buildings, and while it is equally true that many a good lesson has been conducted on the dirt floors of long cabins, it is equally true that rooms can be beautified, and that pleasant surroundings can be made a potent force in holding to our organizations the men and women and boys and girls of the Church. Of course, elaborate, expensive decorations ought to be discouraged. Simplicity always is more consistent with the spirit of worship than is extravagance. But contrast the difference in effect on children of a bare, untidy, makeshift room as against a cozy room decorated with a few beautiful pictures or draperies and made homelike with comfortable seats and tidy arrangement.

Nor is any great expense involved. The writer recalls visiting a kindergarten class in one of the schools in Salt Lake County. The ward authorities had not been asked for a dollar to fit up the room, and yet it had one of the "homiest" atmospheres imaginable. The teacher of the class, in addition to having an interest in the class, had an artistic temperament. She had collected through a number of years the most beautiful pictures that had appeared in the magazines. These in their home-made frames transformed the walls of her room into a veritable art gallery—wherever the eye of the visitor rested, it was greeted by a picture that, through its beauty, drove home an appreciation of the finer things of life. The children, too, had been stimulated to a pride in their room. They had brought in the available old rags from their homes and, as the result of a Sunday School entertainment which they had put on with the co-operation of the other departments of the school, they had had the rags woven into one of those cheerful, old-fashioned home-made carpets. It was perfectly clear that the children took delight in going to this "their room" each Sunday morning. Their pride prompted them to take care of what they regarded as their room, and made for a spirit of quiet and good order hard to surpass.

During the course in teacher-training at Provo, last summer, one of the members of the class courteously took the pains to see that a bouquet of flowers adorned the teacher's desk each day that the class met. It is impossible to estimate the effect of those flowers. Their beauty, coupled with the thoughtfulness that brought them in, made for a "fragrance of spirit" that exerted a remarkable influence.

Once the idea becomes established, pupils will take delight in making their classroom a place in which they will love to meet.

2. *The Teacher.* We have already discussed at length the personality of the teacher and its force in teaching. We need only emphasize the fact here that the magnetism of the teacher, either through what he is or what he gives, is the one great factor that makes for class spirit. The class inevitably reflects the attitude of the man who directs it. He must radiate enthusiasm before it can be caught by his pupils. His inspiration in making them feel that their class is "the one class" of an organization is only too gladly responded to by those whom he teaches. If he impresses the class with the fact that he joins with them because he loves so to do rather than because he has a duty to perform—if he makes suggestions in the interest of a better class—if he starts out by doing something himself by way of a contribution to the class and its spirit—he can be reasonably sure that his class will come more than half-way to join in his plans.

Not only his attitude is a vital factor—his preparation must be of the same enthusiastic type. A pupil of a very successful teacher in Salt Lake City recently made the remark, "I wouldn't think of missing Brother — —'s class. He gives me food for a week." Pressed as to the explanation of this enthusiasm, he added, "Brother — — is unique. He always attacks a subject in such a new and thorough way. He goes below the surface and really teaches us the Gospel." It is not strange, of course, that such advertising on the part of class members has built up an enrollment of some seventy-five pupils. Let us, then, remind ourselves that boys like a teacher

> "Who has pep,"
> "Who tells us something new,"
> "Who doesn't preach at us."

3. *Capitalizing on the Leadership of the Class.* Just as in every band of horses there is a leader, so there is in every group of boys and girls. And as with the leaders, so with the followers. "Get the leaders," says a veteran horseman, "and you have all the rest." It is frequently the case that a teacher does not know intimately all of his pupils. Perhaps in many cases that teacher can know well a few of the outstanding leaders. He can well accompany them on hikes, can take them to a theatre, a ball game, or for a ride. If he wins them they become his lieutenants—they make his class. A word from him and these "under officers" lead the whole class to the

desired reaction. "Take your leading pupils into your confidence and they will establish you in the confidence of all the rest." The experience is related of a teacher sent into southern Utah to take charge of a class of boys who had "dismissed" three teachers already, within the first half year of school. When the newcomer arrived, the air was full of rumblings as to what was to become of number four. He was variously cautioned to make an early departure, to go into school "armed" to "expect anything." But this particular teacher appreciated the fact that he was best armed when backed by the confidence and good will of his class. It was an easy matter to have pointed out for him "the meanest boy of the lot." This boy he sought out and found playing a game of horseshoe. Invited to take a place in the game, he entered the circle of the "outlaws" by winning decisively from their champion—"the meanest boy." To this boy, the new teacher was a "real fellow." Whatever he said, went! The word was circulated overnight among the boys of the town. The teacher already was master of the situation. "The meanest boy," instead of being the chief outlaw, now took pride in being chief lieutenant. Winning the leader won the group, and teacher number four not only stayed the year out, but was petitioned to come back a second year. As a matter of fact, he says, he taught school in that town for seven years.

4. *Putting a Premium on Participation.* One of the most interesting classes the writer has ever visited was a theological class in the Granite Stake. The teacher was committed to the policy of taking as little as possible of the class period himself, but he was also committed to the policy of getting his pupils to do the most possible. For the particular day in question he had assigned a discussion of baptism. One member of the class had been asked to discuss sprinkling as the correct method, another had been assigned immersion. The two young men brought in their findings as if they had been trained for a debate. Within the forty minutes devoted to the recitation baptism had been gone into as thoroughly as the writer has ever seen it gone into during the course of a single lesson, and the members of the class had been delightfully entertained and enlightened. When the bell rang announcing the close of the recitation, the class petitioned to have the discussion continued the following Sunday. It was perfectly clear how the teacher had built up his enrollment.

It is fundamental in human nature to love social combat. The clash of mind versus mind makes a wonderful appeal. Witness a political convention or an open forum debate! Let it be known that a vital subject is to be discussed by men who are really prepared and other men bestir themselves to be in attendance. Surely no subjects are full of more vital significance than questions of life and life eternal. If a teacher will take the pains to select attention-compelling headings and then stimulate representative members of his class really to work out something of a contribution, he need have no fear of the success of his class. Such procedure not only guarantees a good class—it promotes faith on the part of those participating as few other things can. Too frequently we content ourselves with the routine of commonplace "talk." There is no enthusiasm in mere routine as there is none in listless listening to generalities. Our effort should be to make our classes intellectual social centers with everybody participating.

5. *Promoting Class Activities Out of Hours.* The Seventies who harvested the grain for the widow of one of their members did a splendid bit of service, not only for her but for their own quorum. A common objective in service made for a common bond in fellowship.

The Primary class that was stimulated to take a basket of flowers to one of its sick members was helped not only in the making of someone happy, but in building up a class spirit that guaranteed success.

There are so many possibilities open to the teacher who really cares. Just the other evening the teacher of a class of Bee Hive girls called them together for a little social entertainment that they might talk over plans for the approaching season. What a capital attitude? Not to wait till the season opened, but to take the pains to look up the available, prospective class members and make ready for an enthusiastic campaign. Of course, such a teacher will succeed.

Class socials of all sorts, baseball teams, authors' clubs, bits of ward service, visits to institutions of interest—scores of worthy opportunities present themselves always to the teacher who is anxious to build up a genuine class spirit. And that spirit is the one great guarantee of real joy in teaching—it makes a class one which its members will always hold in memory.

Questions and Suggestions—Chapter XXIII

1. Why is it essential that a teacher build up a class spirit?
2. Give three practical suggestions on the subject of beautifying classrooms.
3. Discuss the importance of the attitude of a teacher in promoting class spirit.
4. Point out possible methods for enlisting the co-operation of class leaders.
5. What do you consider your best method of stimulating members to participate in class discussions?
6. What kind of class activities contribute most to the life of your class?
7. Discuss the advisability of promoting class athletic teams.

Helpful References

Colgrove, *The Teacher and the School*; Weigle, *Talks to Sunday School Teachers*; Dewey, *Interest and Effort in Education*; O'Shea, *Everyday Problems in Teaching*; Norsworthy and Whitley, *Psychology of Childhood*.

CHAPTER XXIV

CONVERSION—THE REAL TEST OF TEACHING

Outline—Chapter XXIV

Character, a great power in conversion.—Our concern the converted teacher and also the converted pupil.—The converted teacher believes what he teaches.—The converted teacher practices what he teaches.—The force of "Come, follow me."—What makes for conversion.—The teacher's obligation to kindle the spiritual fire.—His obligation to feature testimony-bearing.—His obligation to take his pupils where they will feel the spirit of testimony.

A number of years ago a young graduate of one of our eastern universities was employed to teach science in a school in Japan. He was employed with the understanding that though he was free to advance whatever scientific theories he chose he should say nothing about his Christian religion. He accepted the conditions gladly, and during the first year of his service was careful not even to mention Christianity. He not only taught his classes in science, but he joined with the boys in their athletics and in their social life generally. Being both an athlete and a leader, he was soon looked to as the life of the school. His clean life was an inspiration. He inevitably set a Christian standard. Before the end of the second year, though he had preached never a word, forty young men made application for membership in his church. His life and ideals had converted them as no preaching could have done.

What was true in this case is inevitably true in the case of all real teachers. What a man is breathes a power of conversion that no force or argument can equal. Hence this concluding chapter—Conversion, the Real Test of Teaching.

First of all, we are concerned with the conversion of the teacher; secondly, with the conversion of the pupil. They are inseparably interwoven. Only the converted teacher can make converts of his pupils. And surely there is very great need of this very thing—*the making of real converts of our boys and girls* that they may come fully to appreciate the significance of the Gospel of Jesus Christ. Upon them rests the carrying forward of that great work which only the *conversion* of our pioneer forefathers could have achieved.

In the first place, the converted teacher *believes* what he teaches. There is no half-hearted attitude toward the subject in hand. To him it is both true and vital. He teaches with a positiveness and an assurance which grip pupils. What a difference between the speech in which a speaker merely makes certain observations—sets forth certain specified facts—and the speech in which those same facts are heightened by that glow of conviction which stamps them as indispensably essential to proper living. The prayer of a man who does not believe in prayer is an example of the emptiness of unbelief. There is one minister in Chicago who openly announces that God does not and can not answer the prayers of mankind. And yet he prays. And what mockery is his praying. Mere words. No man is ever touched by such an empty form. Such prayers have none of that *Heaven Force* which establishes communion with the Lord. Surely "They draw near me with their lips, but their hearts are far from me."

To everyone comes the experience of listening to the heavy phrases of him who would argue and harrangue his auditors into salvation. How his words seem not only to close their minds, but to shut their hearts as well. He fairly talks so loudly that they can't hear him. And then some humble follower of Him who shunned the orator's eloquence moves to tears the same audience by his simple utterance of what he knows and feels to be true. He adds the conviction of conversion to mere "hard-headedness." When a man knows that which he teaches is true there is a spirit that gives power to what he says. "The letter killeth, but the spirit giveth life."

The experience of a Montana railroad executive gives force to this thought. He told one of our leaders how he had always been impressed with the achievements of our Church. In fact, he became such an admirer of the wonderful organization of the "Mormon" Church that he decided to adopt the same kind of organization in his railroad. To quote: "I thought if I could apply the same system up here that you have in the 'Mormon' Church it would work just the same for me as it did for you. I have copied its plan with the First Presidency, the Council of the Twelve, the Presiding Bishop, and all the other officers. I have tried it—but it wouldn't work for me." Only a Latter-day Saint can fully understand why.

And so the teacher who would become a converter must feel the truth of what he teaches so that a spirit of conviction extends from him to his class and so takes hold of the members that they, too, feel the truth of what he says. In short, the real teacher must have a testimony of the truthfulness of the Gospel of Jesus Christ. He must be caught up by that same spirit that opened the heavens to the Prophet Joseph Smith—only then can he really teach. The Lord has so revealed:

> "And they shall observe the covenants and church articles to do them, and these shall be their teaching, as they shall be directed by the Spirit;
>
> "And the Spirit shall be given unto you by the prayer of faith, and if ye receive not the Spirit, ye shall not teach." (Doc. & Cov., Sec. 42:13, 14.)
>
> "Verily I say unto you, he that is ordained of me and sent forth to preach the word of truth by the Comforter, in the Spirit of Truth, doth he preach it by the Spirit of Truth or some other way?

> "And if it be by some other way, it is not of God.
>
> "And again, he that receiveth the word of truth, doth he receive it by the Spirit of Truth or some other way?
>
> "If it be some other way it be not of God:
>
> "Therefore, why is it that ye cannot understand and know that he that receiveth the word by the Spirit of Truth, receiveth it as it is preached by the Spirit of Truth?
>
> "Wherefore, he that preacheth and he that receiveth, understandeth one another, and both are edified and rejoice together;
>
> "And that which doth not edify is not of God and is darkness;
>
> "That which is of God is light; and he that receiveth light and continueth in God, receiveth more light, and that light groweth brighter and brighter until the perfect day." (Doc. & Cov., Sec. 50:17-24.)

In the second place, the teacher's belief must be translated into daily life. "Come, follow me," is the admonition that makes for conversion. A young man recently, in characterizing the biggest failure among teachers that he had ever known, remarked, "He simply couldn't teach us anything. He started in by giving us a vigorous lecture against tobacco, but before a week had passed we all knew that he himself smoked. He might just as well have given up teaching right there. We couldn't see any truth in him after that, for the 'smoke' of his own deception."

Of course, he was not converted. A similar experience is related of the principal of a school who, with his faculty of teachers, made it a school rule that there should be no playing of cards on the part of the students. The rule recorded, however, the principal proceeded to participate in downtown card parties until he established a reputation, in the language of the boys, as a "card shark." Not only did that principal find it impossible thereafter to combat the evil of students cutting classes to play cards, he lost that confidence on the part of the student body without which school discipline cannot be achieved. Lack of conversion—such conversion as leads a man to practice what he preaches—cost him his position.

To the teacher who would develop the power of conversion, may we make reference by way of review to those suggestions in an earlier chapter that make for spiritual growth:

1. Live a clean life.
2. Read the word of the Lord.
3. Do the duties assigned by those in authority.
4. Subscribe to all the principles of the Gospel.
5. Cultivate a real spirit of prayer.

If the teacher is really converted, of course the conversion of his pupils follows very largely as a corollary. But by way of practical suggestion, it may be helpful to list some things that may be done to promote a spirit of testimony on the part of the pupils. At the outset a teacher ought to appreciate just what a testimony is and how it varies with the age and experience of children. It is clearly a mistake as a general rule to expect young children to give expression to a testimony such as might be borne by an adult. True, some children enjoy at an early age the spirit of testimony to such an extent that they do seem to know that the Gospel is true. But it is wiser not to expect too much. Then, too, testimonies vary with individuals. Teachers ought to look out for expressions which are characteristic of the pupil in question rather than to expect all pupils to measure up to a set standard.

With a proper conception of a testimony, the teacher then owes certain rather definite obligations to his class.

He ought to feature testimony bearing rather than to apologize for it. In the teaching of the Gospel of Jesus Christ there can be no more sacred opportunity than that which allows pupils to open their hearts to their Creator.

Then, too, the teacher owes it to his class to *kindle* the spiritual fire which alone can make for testimony bearing. Brother Maeser had a very effective way of illustrating the significance of this obligation. As he expressed the thought, no one would feel that he had completed his task of warming a house if he merely put into the grate the necessary paper, wood and coal. He might have all these, but until he struck the match which would kindle the fire, no warmth would be felt. And so, spiritually, the fire of a testimony-meeting needs to be kindled. All too often, a teacher opens the class hour with some such statement as this, "Now, boys and girls, today is Fast Day. I hope you won't let the time go to waste." What inspiration in such an opening! That teacher has not only not kindled the fire, he has brought in a lump or two of coal—hard at that—with no kindling even as a promise of a fire. On the other hand, the successful teacher comes before his class with a vital truth that thrills him and gives it a concrete expression which prompts pupils to add similar experiences out of their own lives.

Then, too, the teacher may well bring into his class by way of inspiration someone well established in the faith whose experiences are full of the spirit of conversion. There are in every ward in the Church those men and women who know of a surety that the gospel is true. Why not bring them in occasionally to stimulate testimony bearing? Might it not be well, also, to take the class as a class to our Fast Day Sacrament service, there to let them enjoy the wonderful spirit of testimony that is so characteristic of these meetings? There is a feeling of conversion that attends these meetings that all boys and girls must feel—must feel so keenly that they in turn will want to give expression to their own convictions.

And finally, as teachers, let us remind ourselves that in this matter of promoting the bearing of testimonies we should exercise a patience that is full of tolerance and forbearance. Some few individuals are converted suddenly; others respond to the truth gradually; and there are those who do well if they really respond to the feeling of conversion at the end of a lifetime. As one of our leaders has so beautifully pointed out, the Master, Himself, did not convert the world in a day, nor a year—He has not converted it in all these centuries. His plan seems to be to teach the truth and wait patiently until the divinity in man asserts itself—until man walks by his own light into eternal truth. Under the inspiration of such example may teachers well labor on in earnestness, happy in the thought that He will hasten in His own due time what to them may seem a long, slow process.

> "Perchance, in heaven, one day to me
> Some blessed Saint will come and say,
> 'All hail, beloved; but for thee
> My soul to death had fallen a prey';
> And oh! what rapture in the thought,
> One soul to glory to have brought."

Questions and Suggestions—Chapter XXIV

1. Why is conversion the real test of religious teaching?
2. What are the outstanding characteristics of a person newly converted to the Church?
3. Discuss the significance of each of the factors that make for conversion.
4. Illustrate how to kindle the spiritual fire.
5. State why or why not you favor making assignments for testimony day.
6. What is a testimony?
7. How may children best cultivate a testimony?
8. What principle or practice means most to you by way of affirming your own testimony?

Helpful References

The Doctrine & Covenants, The Bible, The Book of Mormon, The Voice of Warning, Rays of Living Light.

BIBLIOGRAPHY

The Art of Teaching	Driggs	Deseret Book Co., Salt Lake.
The Art of Questioning	Fitch	A. Flanigan Co., Chicago.
Story Telling, Questioning and Studying	Horne	MacMillan Co., New York.
Principles of Psychology	James	H. Holt & Co., New York.
Fundamentals of Child Study	Kirkpatrick	MacMillan Co., New York.
A Study of Child Nature	Harrison	R.R. Donnelley & Sons, Chicago.
Psychology of Childhood	Norsworthy and Whitley	MacMillan Co., New York.
The Essentials of Character	Sisson	MacMillan Co., New York.
Principles of Teaching	Thorndike	A.G. Seiler, New York.
Education for Character	Sharp	Bobbs, Merrill Co., Indianapolis.
The Ideal Teacher	G.H. Palmer	Houghton-Mifflin Co., New York.
The Seven Laws of Teaching	J.M. Gregory	The Pilgrim Press, Chicago.
The Point of Contact in Teaching	Dubois	Dodd, Mead & Co., New York.
Interest and Effort in Education	Dewey	Houghton-Mifflin Co., New York.
The Boy Problem	Forbush	The Pilgrim Press, Chicago.
Training the Boy	McKeever	MacMillan Co., New York.
Types of Teaching	Earhart	Houghton-Mifflin Co., New York.
How to Teach Religion	Betts	The Abingdon Press, New York.
Talks to Sunday School Teachers	Weigle	Doran Publishing Co., New York.
Everyday Problems in Teaching	O'Shea	Bobbs, Merrill Co., Indianapolis.
Talks to Teachers	James	H. Holt & Co., New York.
How to Teach	Strayer and Norsworthy	MacMillan Co., New York.
The Making of a Teacher	Brumbaugh	Sunday School Times Co., Phila.

The Learning Process	Colvin	MacMillan Co., New York.
The Teacher and the School	Colgrove	Chas. Scribner & Co., New York.
Pictures in Religious Education	Beard	Geo. H. Doran Co., New York.
The Nervous System	Stiles	W.B. Saunders Co., Phila.
The Classroom Teacher	Strayer and Englehardt	American Book Co., New York.
The Recitation	Betts	Houghton-Mifflin Co., New York.
Attention	Pillsbury	MacMillan Co., New York.
Religious Education in the Family	Cope	University of Chicago Press.
Classroom Method and Management	Betts	Bobbs, Merrill Co., Indianapolis.
Classroom Management	Bagley	MacMillan Co., New York.

9 789361 385452

Printed by Libri Plureos GmbH in Hamburg,
Germany